Three-Octave Scales
for the violin

book one: learning the scales

by Cassia Harvey

edited by Myanna Harvey

CHP354

©2019 by C. Harvey Publications All Rights Reserved.

www.learnstrings.com - downloadable books
www.charveypublications.com - print books

Table of Contents, Page One

Section	Page
How This Book Works	4
How to Use This Book	5
Half and Whole Steps as Building Blocks	6
Playing Whole and Half Steps in This Book	7

Part One: Major Scales, Main Fingering

- G major 8
- A-flat major 10
- A major 12
- B-flat major 14
- B major 16
- C major 18
- D-flat major 20
- D major 22
- E-flat major 24
- E major 26
- F major 28
- F-sharp major 30

Part Two: Minor Scales, Main Fingering

- G minor 32
- G-sharp minor 33
- A minor 34
- B-flat minor 35
- B minor 36
- C minor 37
- C-sharp minor 38
- D minor 39
- E-flat minor 40
- E minor 41
- F minor 42
- F-sharp minor 43

Part Three: Chromatic Scale, Main Fingering — 44
Part Four: Major Scales for Speed — 46
Part Five: Minor Scales for Speed — 58

©2019 C. Harvey Publications All Rights Reserved.

Table of Contents, Page Two

Section	Page
Part Six: Major Scales, Alternate Fingering	
G major	64
A-flat major	66
A major	68
B-flat major	70
B major	72
C major	74
D-flat major	76
D major	78
E-flat major	80
E major	82
F major	84
F-sharp major	86
Part Seven: Minor Scales, Alternate Fingering	
G minor	88
G-sharp minor	89
A minor	90
B-flat minor	91
B minor	92
C minor	93
C-sharp minor	94
D minor	95
E-flat minor	96
E minor	97
F minor	98
F-sharp minor	99
Part Eight: Chromatic Scale, Alternate Fingering	100
Part Nine: Exercises for Universal Fingering	103
Part Ten: Major Scales with Universal Fingering	121
Part Eleven: Melodic Minor Scales with Universal Fingering	124
Part Twelve: Harmonic Minor Scales with Universal Fingering	127
Part Thirteen: Complete Scales, Main Fingering	130
Part Fourteen: Complete Scales, Alternate Fingering	139

How This Book Works

- Each scale is taught using spacing exercises and shifting exercises.

- When you see this figure, a **space** between two notes is being taught:

- When you see this figure inside repeat signs, a **shift** is being taught:

- The **shifts** are taught through exercises that *use notes you already know to help you find the new notes*. In this example, by playing third finger, you can see and hear how far to shift.

- In this book, Roman numerals refer to strings (not positions):
  I = E string, II = A string, III = D string, IV = G string

Reading Very High Notes with 8va

- When the notes go too high on the staff to comfortably read, a notation is used to make them easier to read. When you see this sign, play the notes under it one octave (eight notes) higher:

Here is an example of how 8va is used in this book:

This is how those same notes would look if written without the 8va:

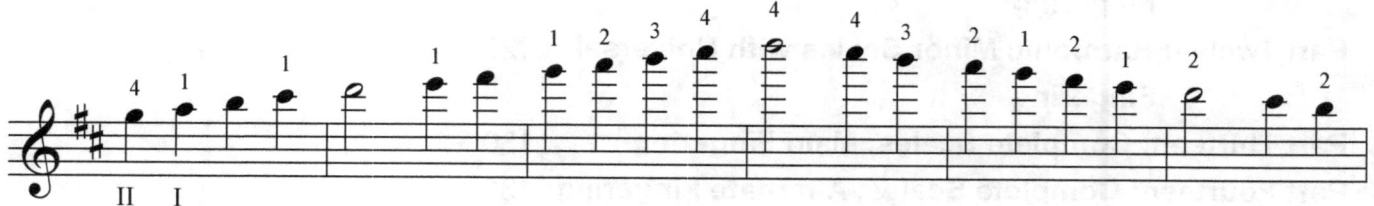

©2019 C. Harvey Publications All Rights Reserved.

How to Use This Book

- Study two pages at a time to learn each major scale and one page at a time to learn each minor scale.

- As you practice, focus on remembering both the spaces and the correct sounds of the scale.

- Repeat shifts until they are played precisely and perfectly in tune.

- Since you are teaching yourself the spaces with quite a bit of repetition, be very careful to place your fingers correctly so that you don't inadvertently build bad habits.

- Play with clean finger articulation to get the most precise intonation.

- Listen for an even tone; play with long, strong bows.

- **Some of the exercises and scales might be most helpful when played with a drone.** The root note, or first note of the scale, is typically the most helpful note to use as a drone. There are apps and websites that have drones to play with; search for *music practice drone*.

What Comes Next

Learning to play scales is just the beginning! A well-rounded daily practice routine should nearly always include scales in some form. However, just playing scales in quarter or eighth notes limits how much the scales can help you improve.

That's where scale variations are valuable. By practicing rhythm, bow, and note variations on scales, both the left and right hands can be trained at the same time.

When you study scale variations, your practice becomes more efficient as the scope of the scales is expanded to teach an almost limitless variety of violin techniques.

Check out www.charveypublications.com for scale variation books and blog posts with free scale variations.

Half Steps and Whole Steps: The Building Blocks of Scales

- Western music is based on a system of whole and half steps (also called tones and semitones) that, when put together in a specific way, form a scale.
- Below are the spaces that make up the scales in this book. Starting with the first note in the scale, you could figure out how to play scales anywhere on the violin by playing the steps indicated.

Major Scale

first note | whole step | whole step | half step | whole step | whole step | whole step | half step

Melodic Minor Scale

going up the scale

first note | whole step | half step | whole step | whole step | whole step | whole step | half step

coming down the scale

whole step | whole step | half step | whole step | whole step | half step | whole step

Harmonic Minor Scale

first note | whole step | half step | whole step | whole step | half step | 1 1/2 steps | half step

Chromatic Scale

first note | half step | half step | half step | half step | half step | half step | half step | half step | half step | half step | half step | half step

©2019 C. Harvey Publications All Rights Reserved.

Three-Octave Scales for the Violin, Book One

Playing Whole and Half Steps

Here are some practical ways to think of steps on the violin:

• When two fingers are next to each other with no space between them, you have reached a half step.

• When there is space for one extra finger between your two fingers, you have reached a whole step.

• As you move up through the positions, the spaces between the notes get smaller. A half step in first position will be much bigger than a half step in seventh position.

• Past 6th or 7th position, your fingers will be very close together but you will still need to listen for the whole and half steps.

In this book, **half steps** are marked this way:

Whole steps are marked this way:

Reaching 1 1/2 Steps in Harmonic Minor Scales

• Harmonic minor scales have spaces of 1 1/2 steps. To reach these spaces, stretch to reach the notes.

• Here are two exercises to help you work on the stretch. These patterns can be applied to other 1 1/2 step stretches as well.

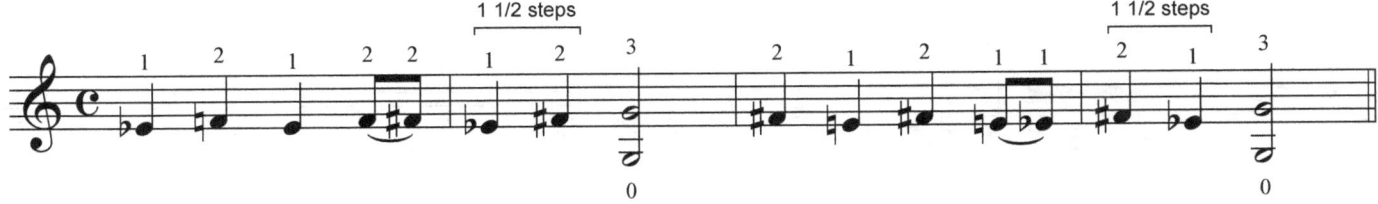

©2019 C. Harvey Publications All Rights Reserved.

Part One: Major Scales, Main Fingering

1. G major - Preparatory Shifting

Cassia Harvey

Three-Octave Scales for the Violin, Book One   Major Scales, Main Fingering   9

E minor is No. 34
G minor is No. 25

2. G major

©2019 C. Harvey Publications All Rights Reserved.

3. A♭ major - Preparatory Shifting

Three-Octave Scales for the Violin, Book One　　　　　　　　　　　　　　Major Scales, Main Fingering　11

4. A♭ major

F minor is No. 35
G♯ minor is No. 26

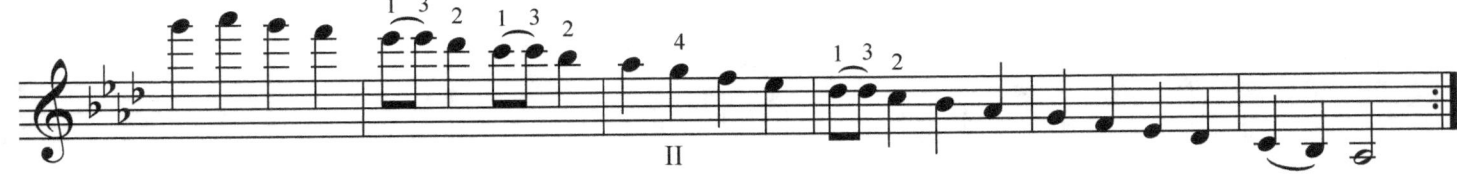

©2019 C. Harvey Publications All Rights Reserved.

5. A major - Preparatory Shifting

7. B♭ major - Preparatory Shifting

9. B major - Preparatory Shifting

Three-Octave Scales for the Violin, Book One | Major Scales, Main Fingering | 17

10. B major

G♯ minor is No. 26
B minor is No. 29

©2019 C. Harvey Publications All Rights Reserved.

11. C major - Preparatory Shifting

Three-Octave Scales for the Violin, Book One Major Scales, Main Fingering 19

12. C major

A minor is No. 27
C minor is No. 30

Scale with shifting guide notes

©2019 C. Harvey Publications All Rights Reserved.

13. D♭ major - Preparatory Shifting

Three-Octave Scales for the Violin, Book One　　　　　　　　　　Major Scales, Main Fingering　21

14. D♭ major

B♭ minor is No. 28
C♯ minor is No. 31

Scale with shifting guide notes

©2019 C. Harvey Publications All Rights Reserved.

15. D major - Preparatory Shifting

Three-Octave Scales for the Violin, Book One Major Scales, Main Fingering   23

16. D major

B minor is No. 29
D minor is No. 32

©2019 C. Harvey Publications All Rights Reserved.

17. E♭ major - Preparatory Shifting

19. E major - Preparatory Shifting

21. F major - Preparatory Shifting

23. F# major - Preparatory Shifting

Part Two: Minor Scales, Main Fingering

B♭ major is No. 8
G major is No. 2

25. G minor

Preparatory Shifting

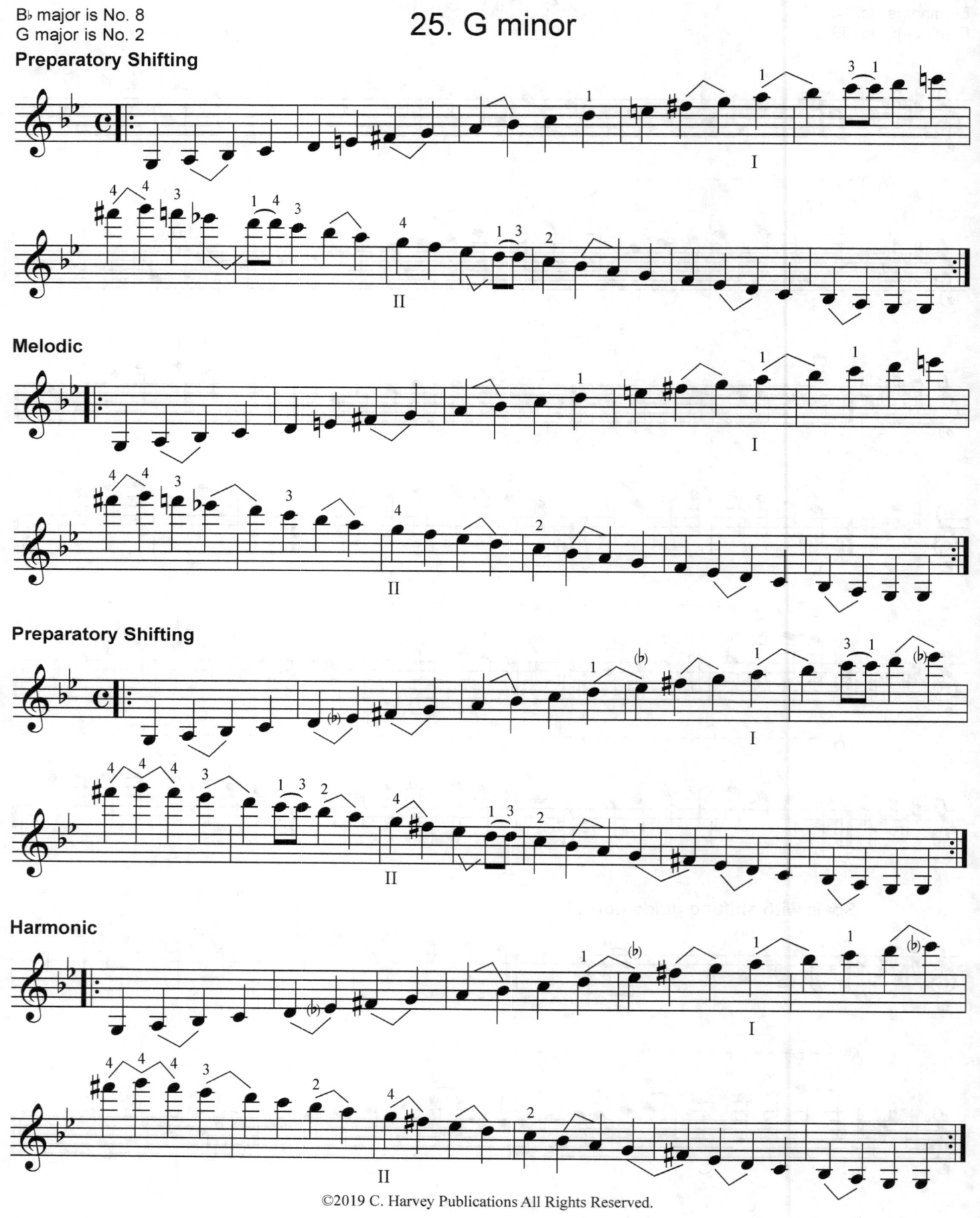

Melodic

Preparatory Shifting

Harmonic

Three-Octave Scales for the Violin, Book One — Minor Scales, Main Fingering — 33

B major is No. 10
A♭ major is No. 4

26. G♯ minor

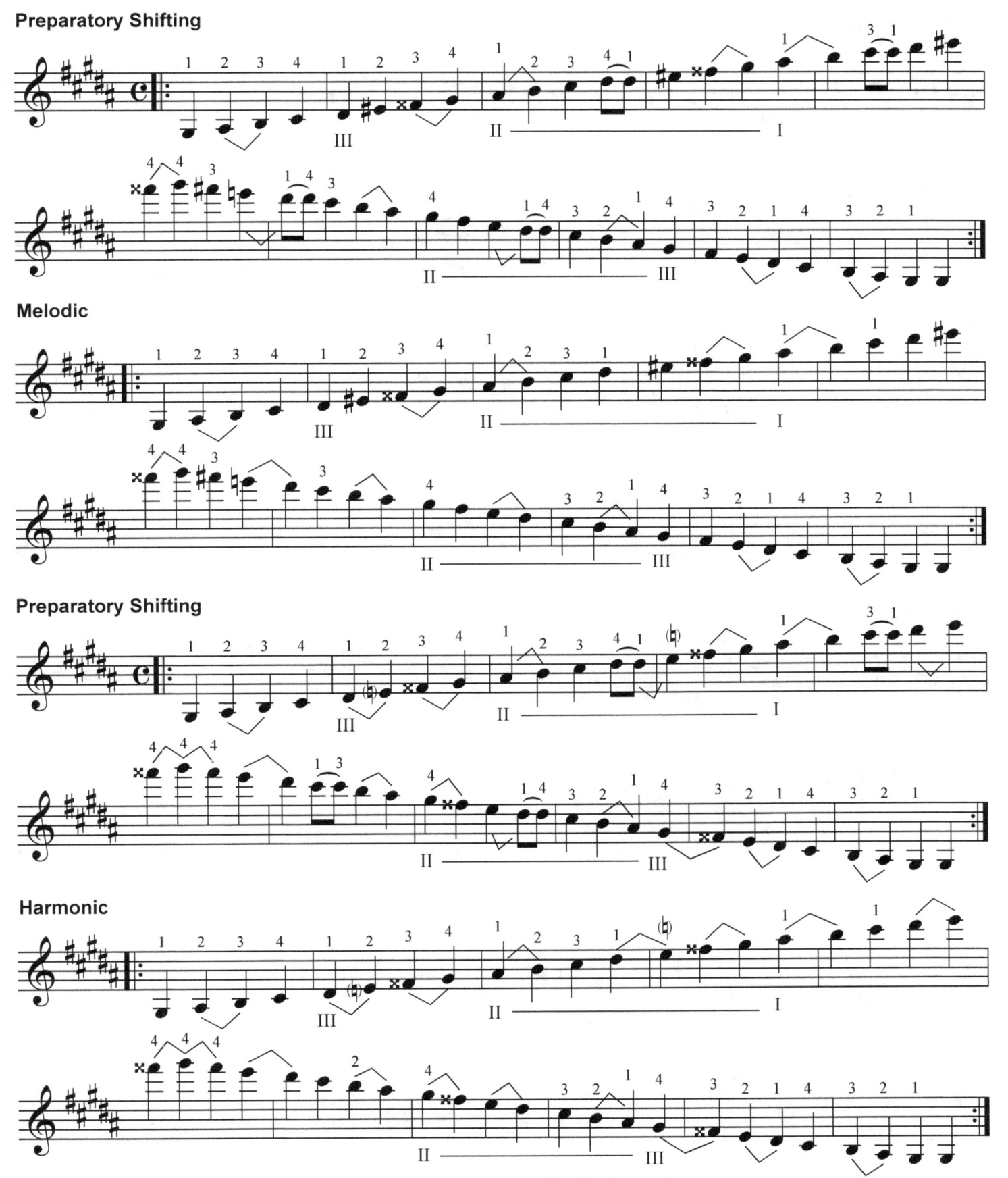

Preparatory Shifting

Melodic

Preparatory Shifting

Harmonic

©2019 C. Harvey Publications All Rights Reserved.

36 Minor Scales, Main Fingering

D major is No. 16
B major is No. 10

29. B minor

Three-Octave Scales for the Violin, Book One   Minor Scales, Main Fingering   37

E♭ major is No. 18
C major is No. 12

30. C minor

©2019 C. Harvey Publications All Rights Reserved.

38 Minor Scales, Main Fingering
Three-Octave Scales for the Violin, Book One

E major is No. 20
D♭ major is No. 14

31. C♯ minor

Preparatory Shifting

Melodic

Preparatory Shifting

Harmonic

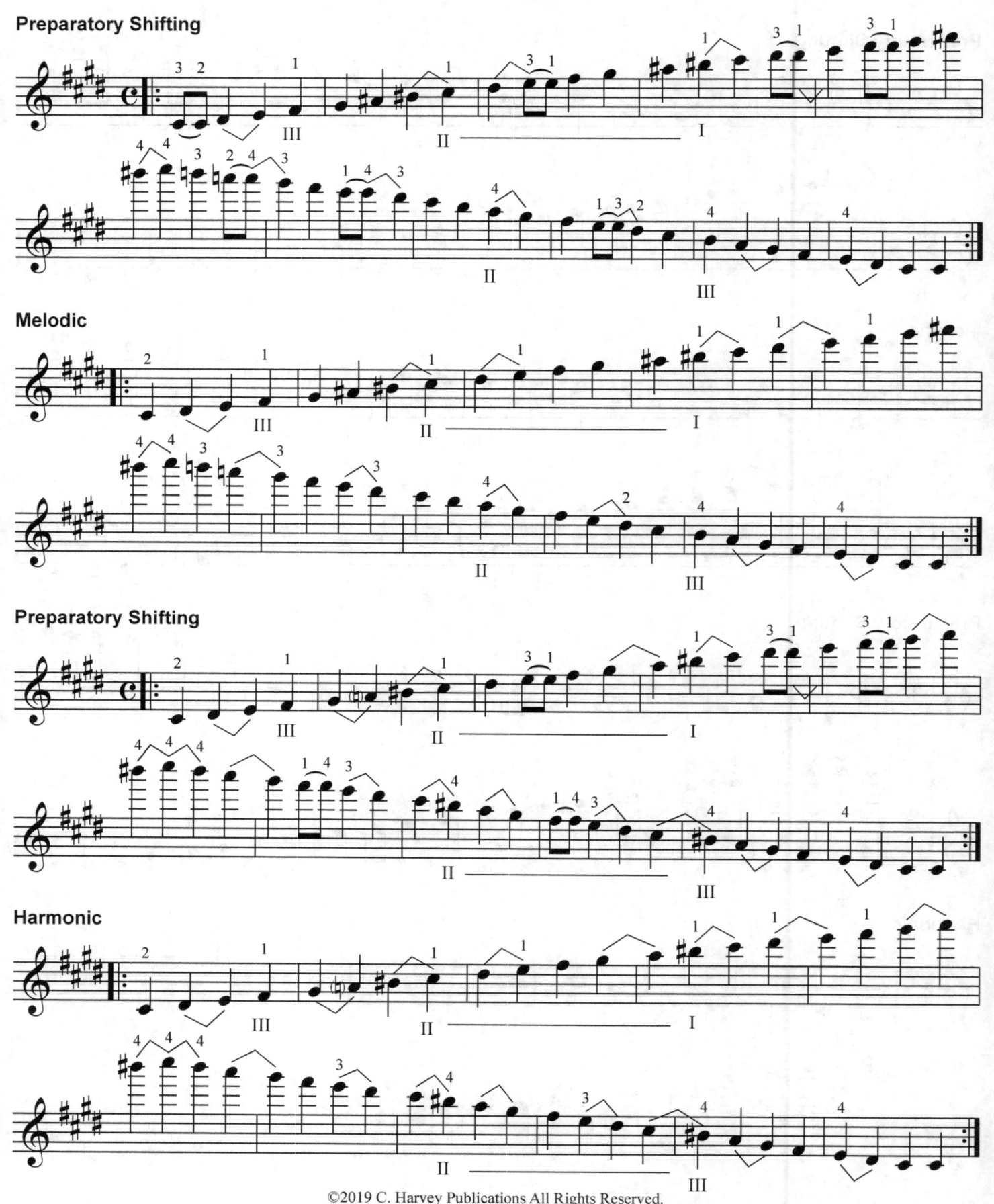

©2019 C. Harvey Publications All Rights Reserved.

Three-Octave Scales for the Violin, Book One — Minor Scales, Main Fingering — 39

F major is No. 22
D major is No. 16

32. D minor

©2019 C. Harvey Publications All Rights Reserved.

40 Minor Scales, Main Fingering — Three-Octave Scales for the Violin, Book One

F# major is No. 24
Eb major is No. 18

33. Eb minor

Preparatory Shifting

Melodic

Preparatory Shifting

Harmonic

©2019 C. Harvey Publications All Rights Reserved.

Three-Octave Scales for the Violin, Book One Minor Scales, Main Fingering 41

G major is No. 2
E major is No. 20

34. E minor

©2019 C. Harvey Publications All Rights Reserved.

Three-Octave Scales for the Violin, Book One — Minor Scales, Main Fingering — 43

A major is No. 6
F# major is No. 24

36. F# minor

Part Three: Chromatic Scale, Main Fingering

37. Chromatic Scale Shifting

Shifting on the E string

Shifting on all strings

38. Chromatic Scale with Slur Patterns

Part Four: Major Scales for Speed

39. G major

40. A♭ major

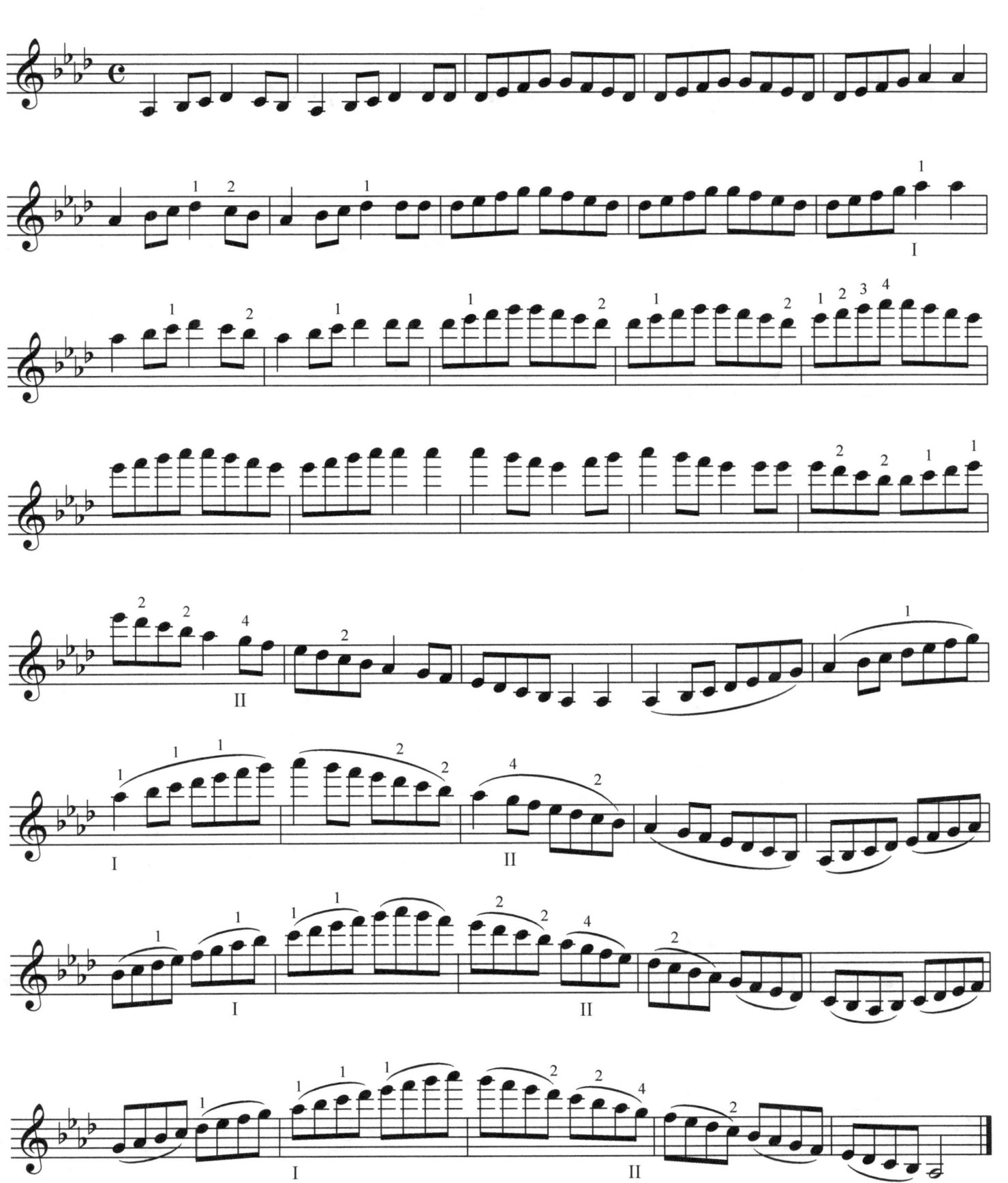

41. A major

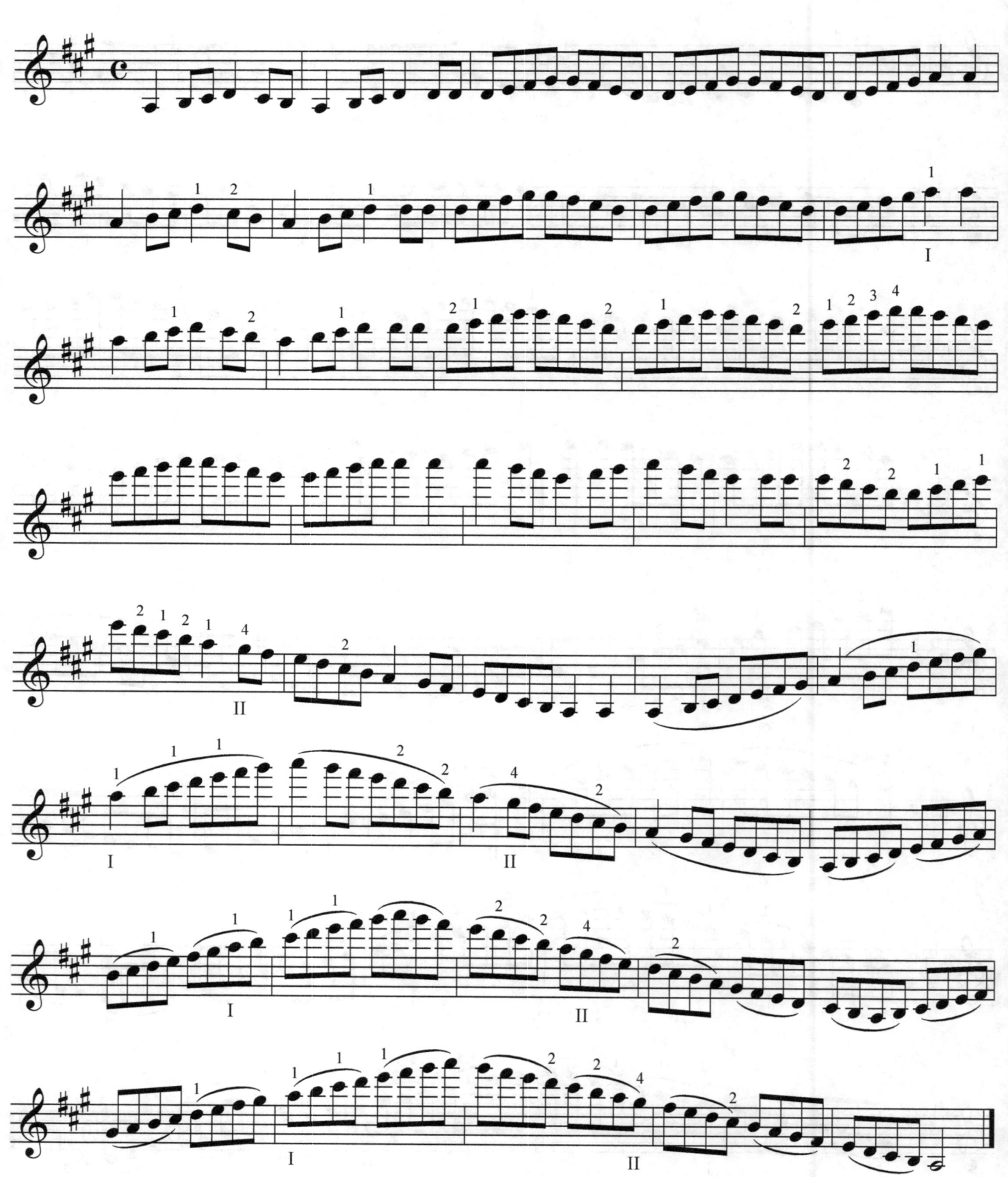

42. B♭ major

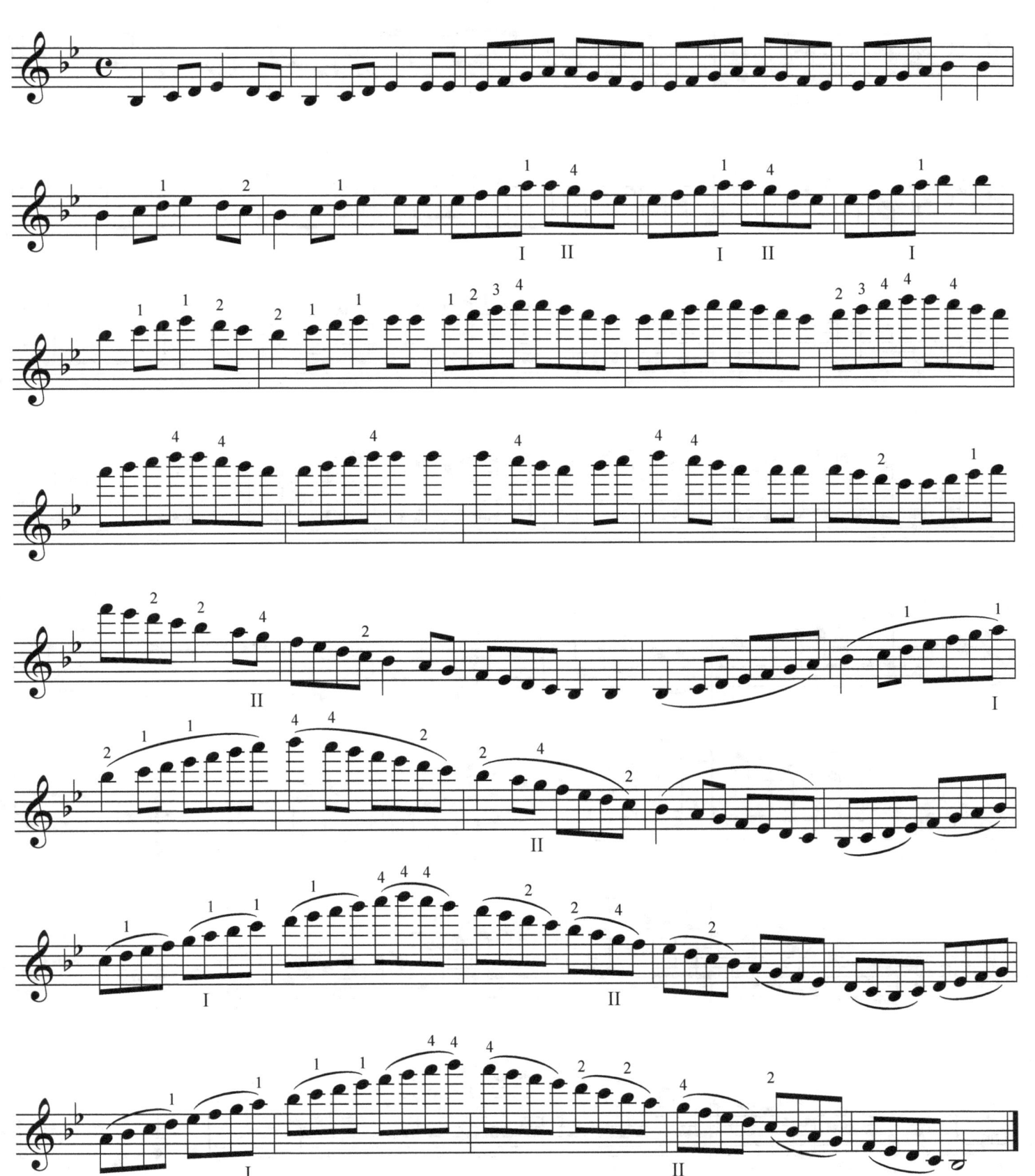

43. B major

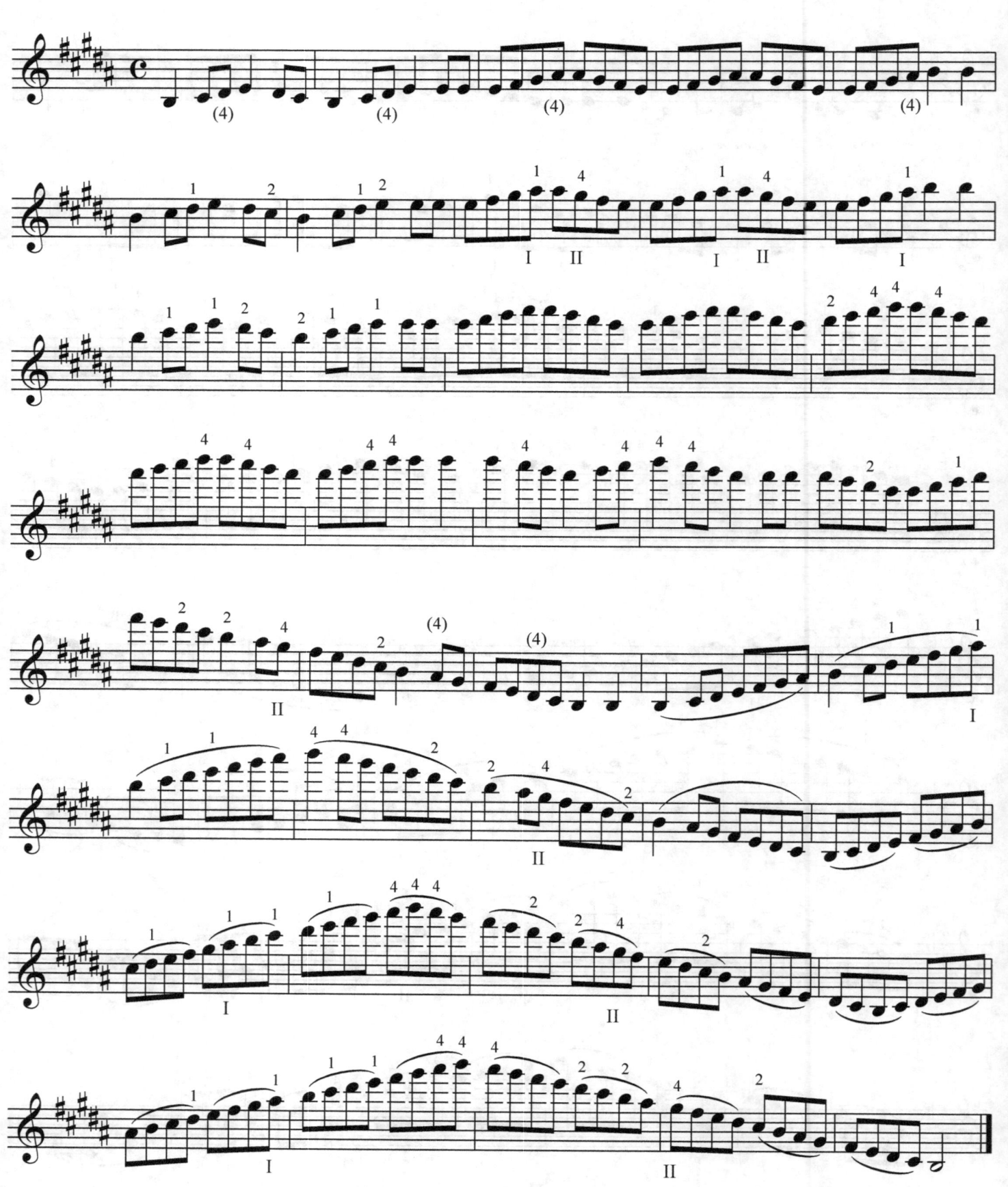

44. C major

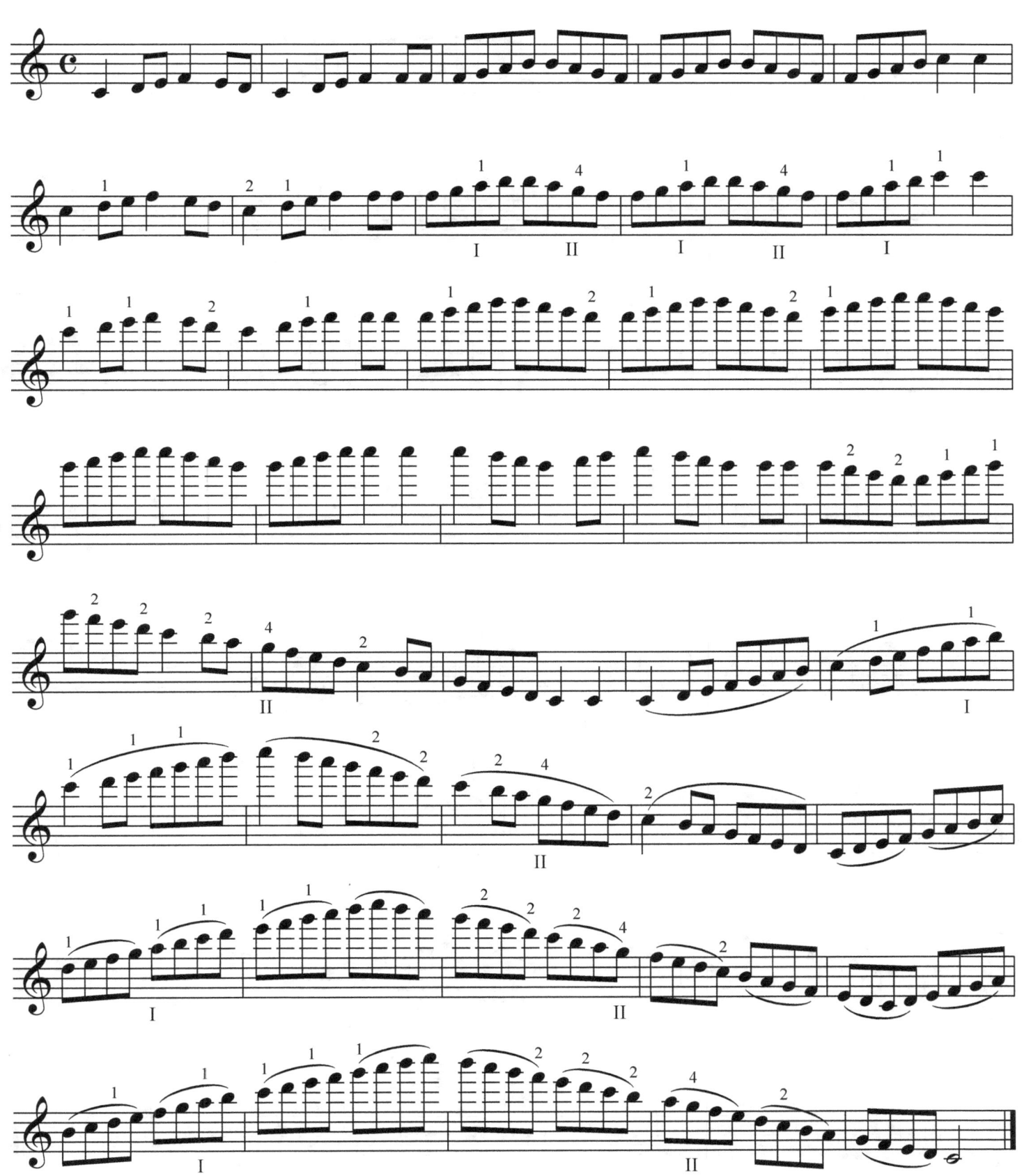

45. D♭ major

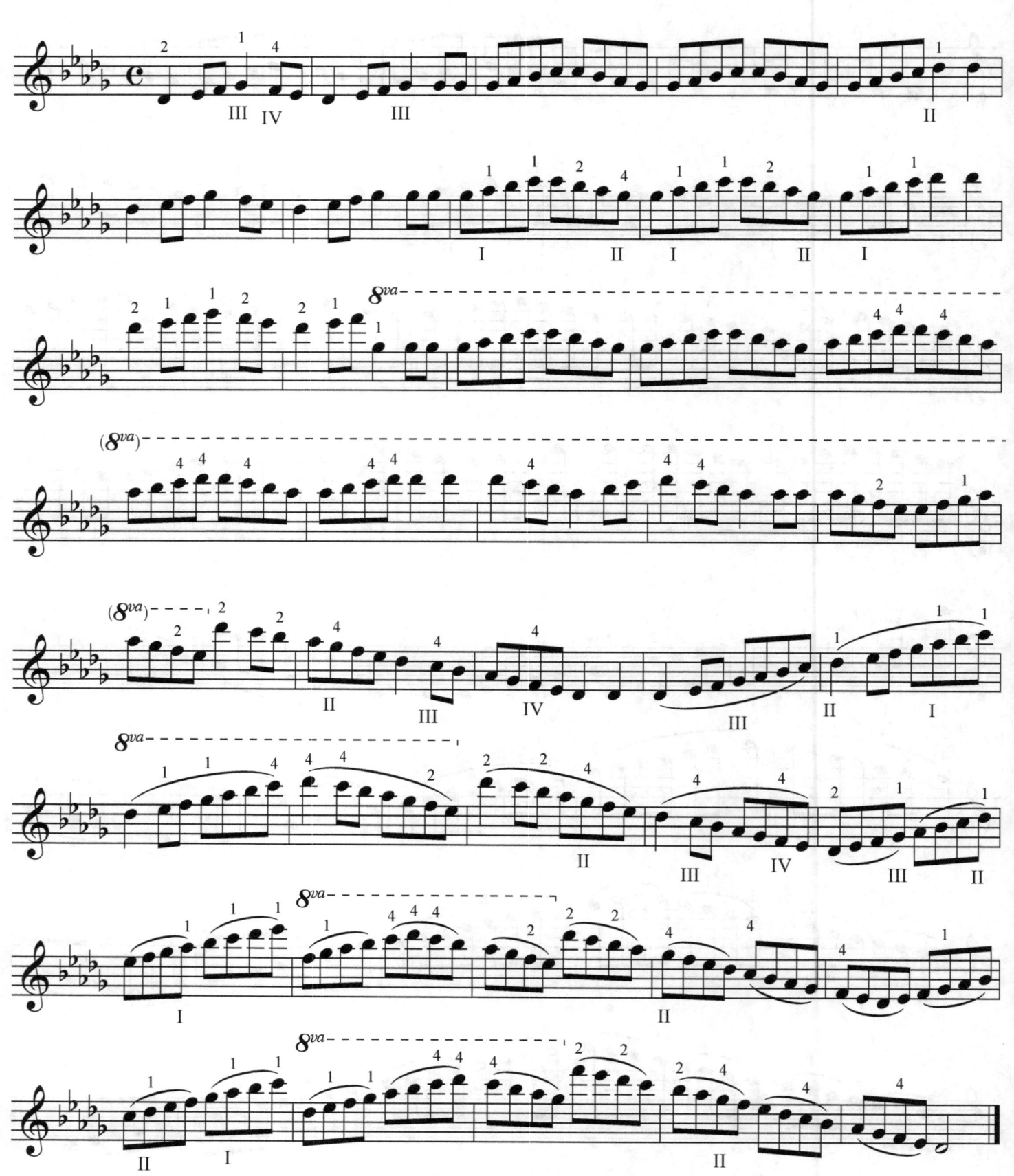

46. D major

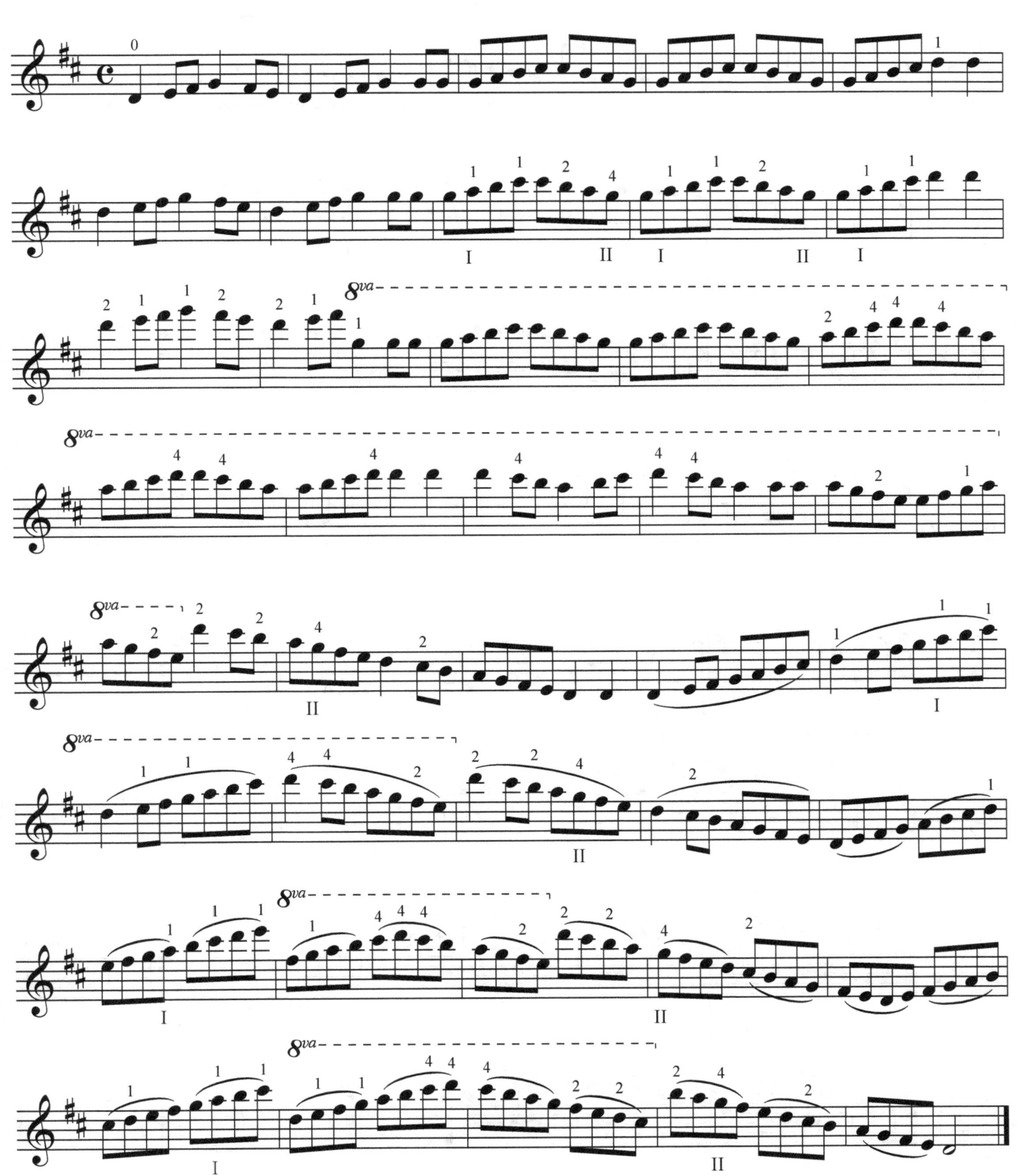

47. E♭ major

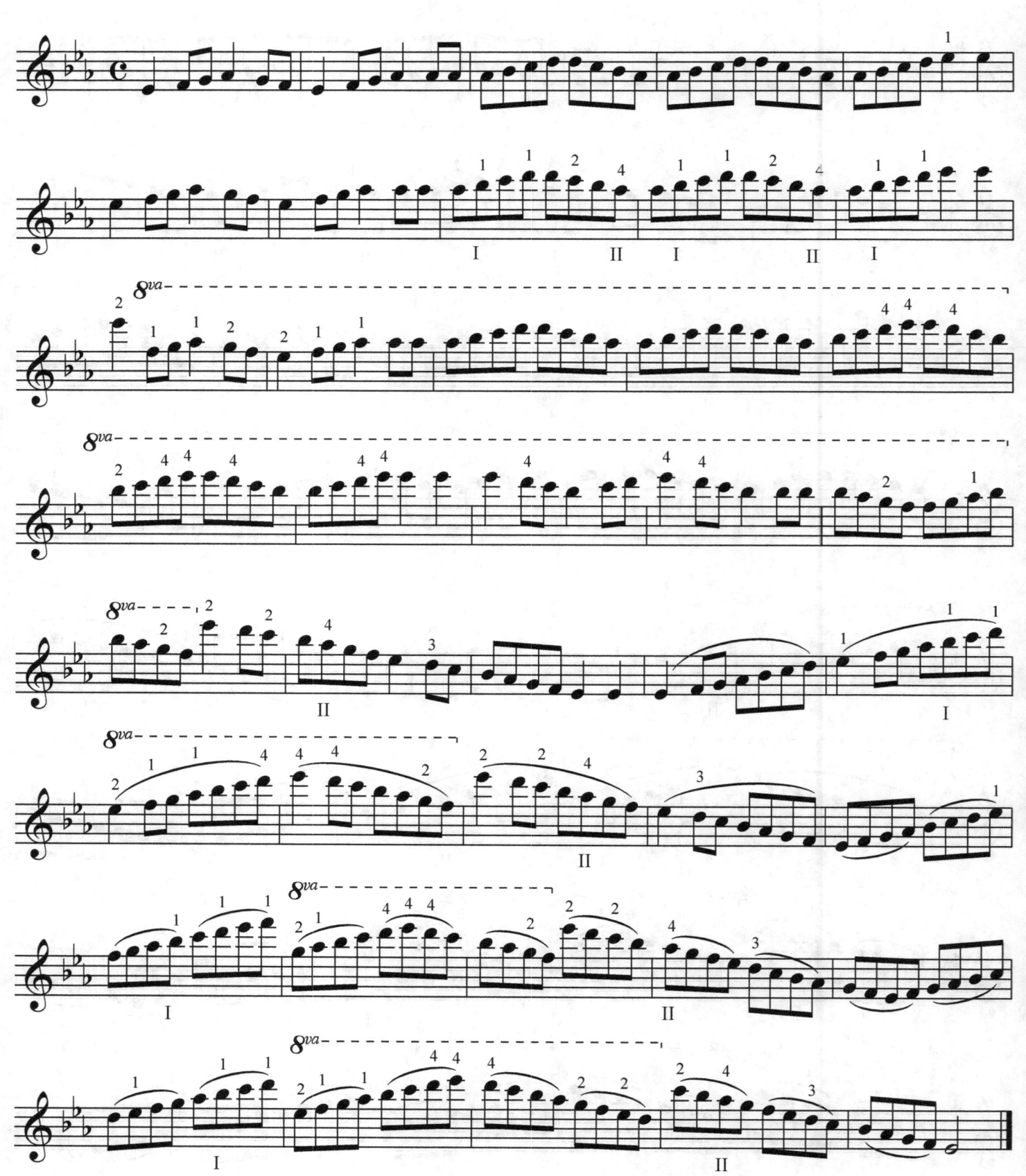

48. E major

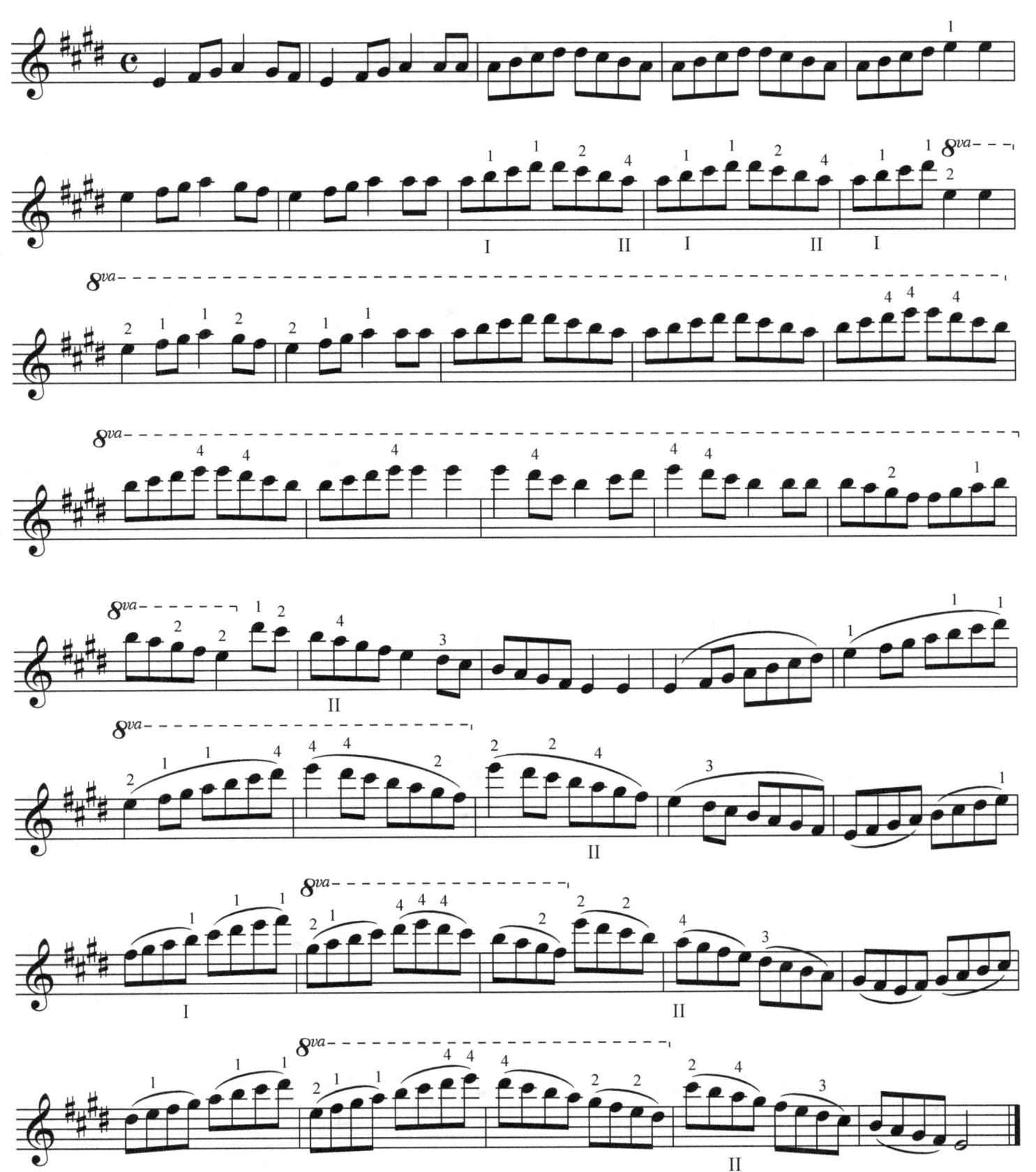

49. F major

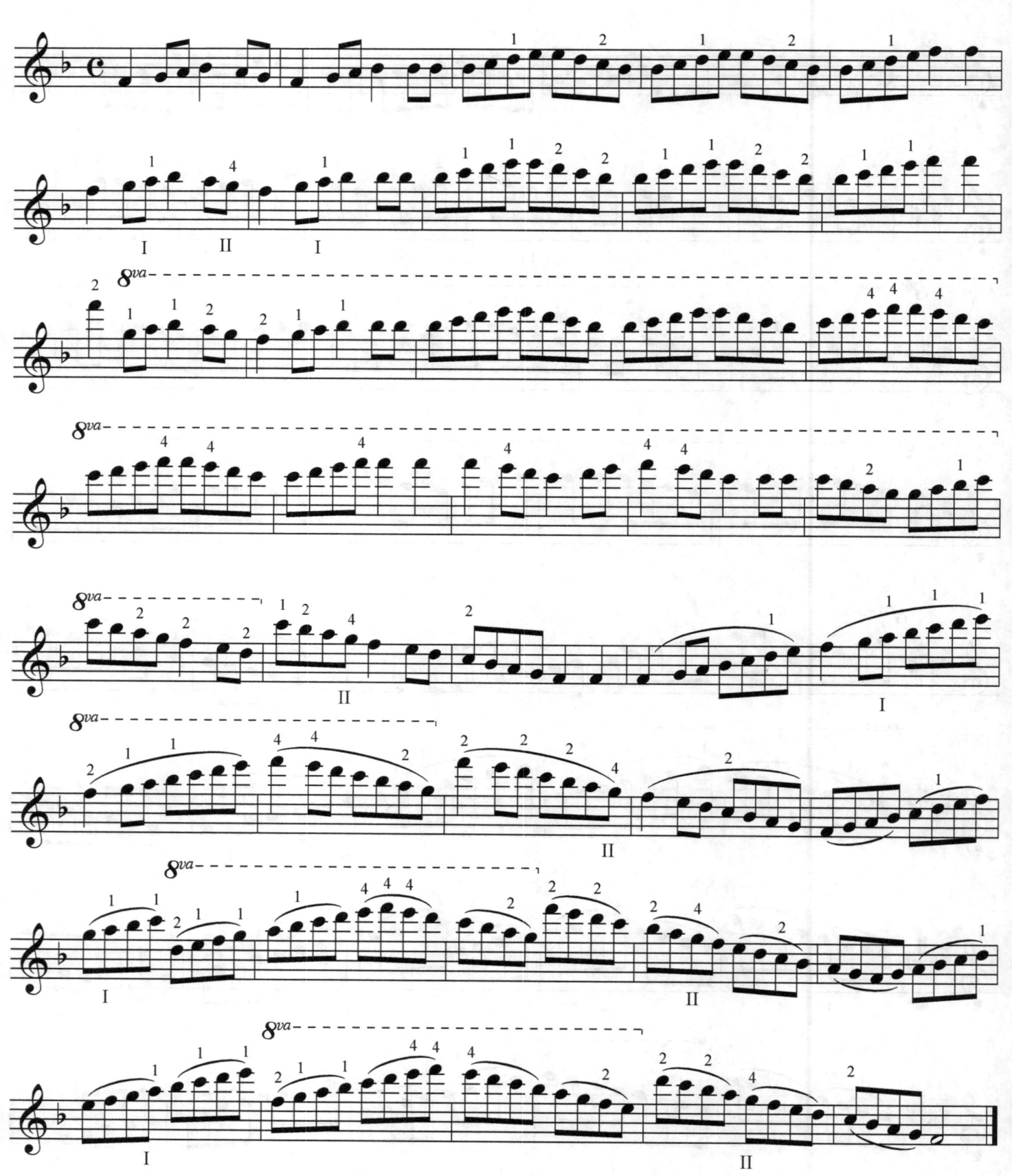

50. F# major

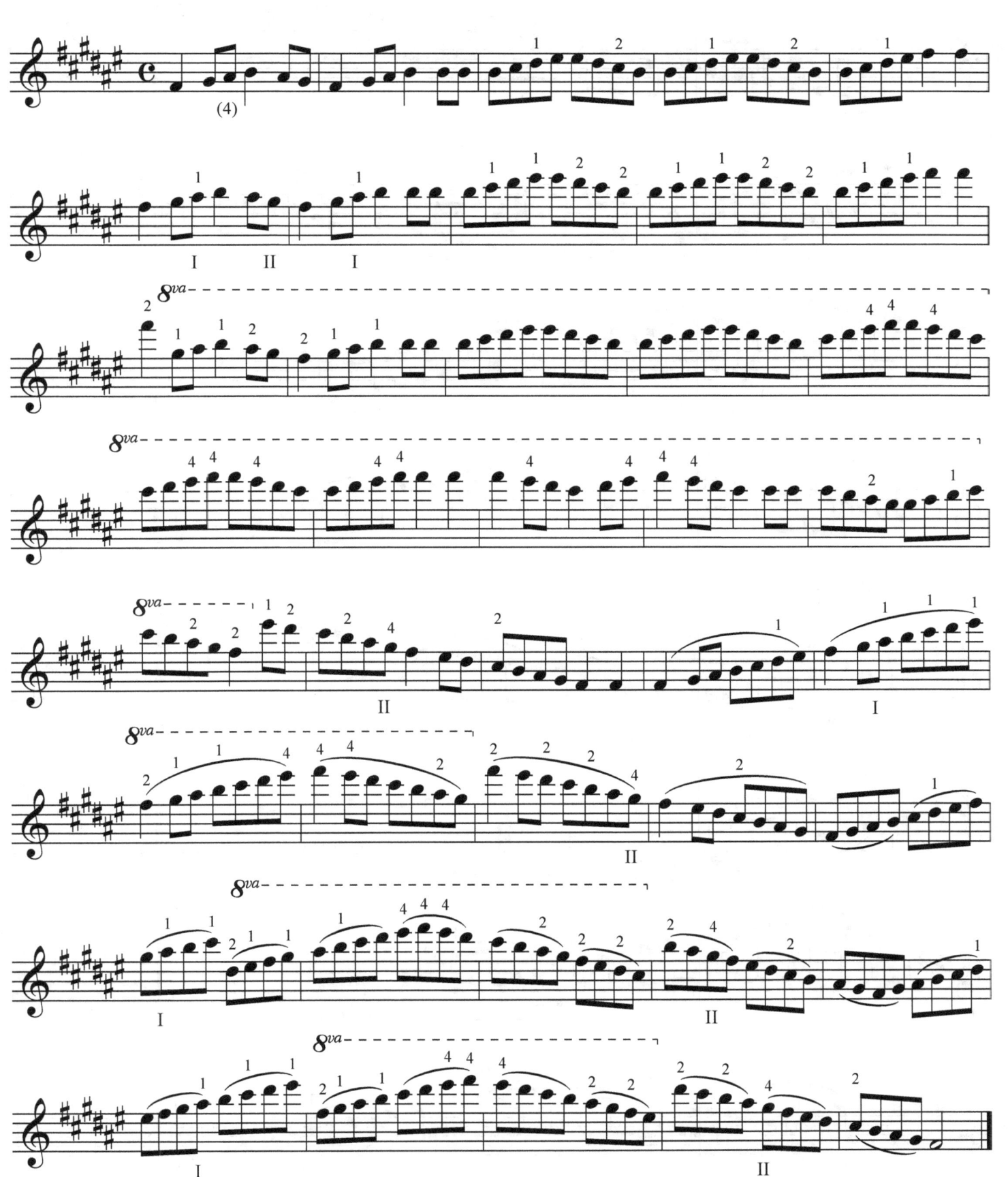

Part Five: Minor Scales for Speed
51. G minor
52. G# minor

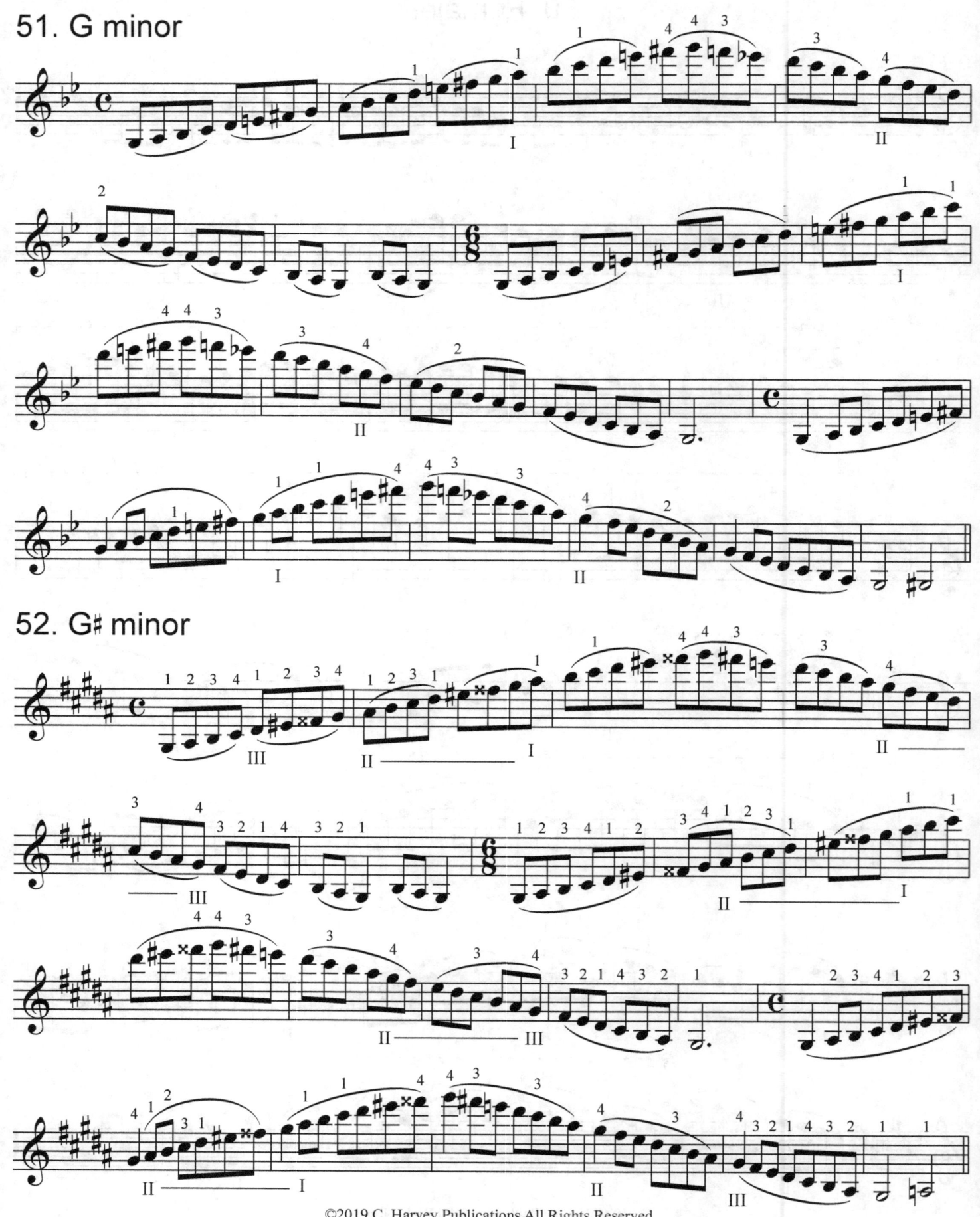

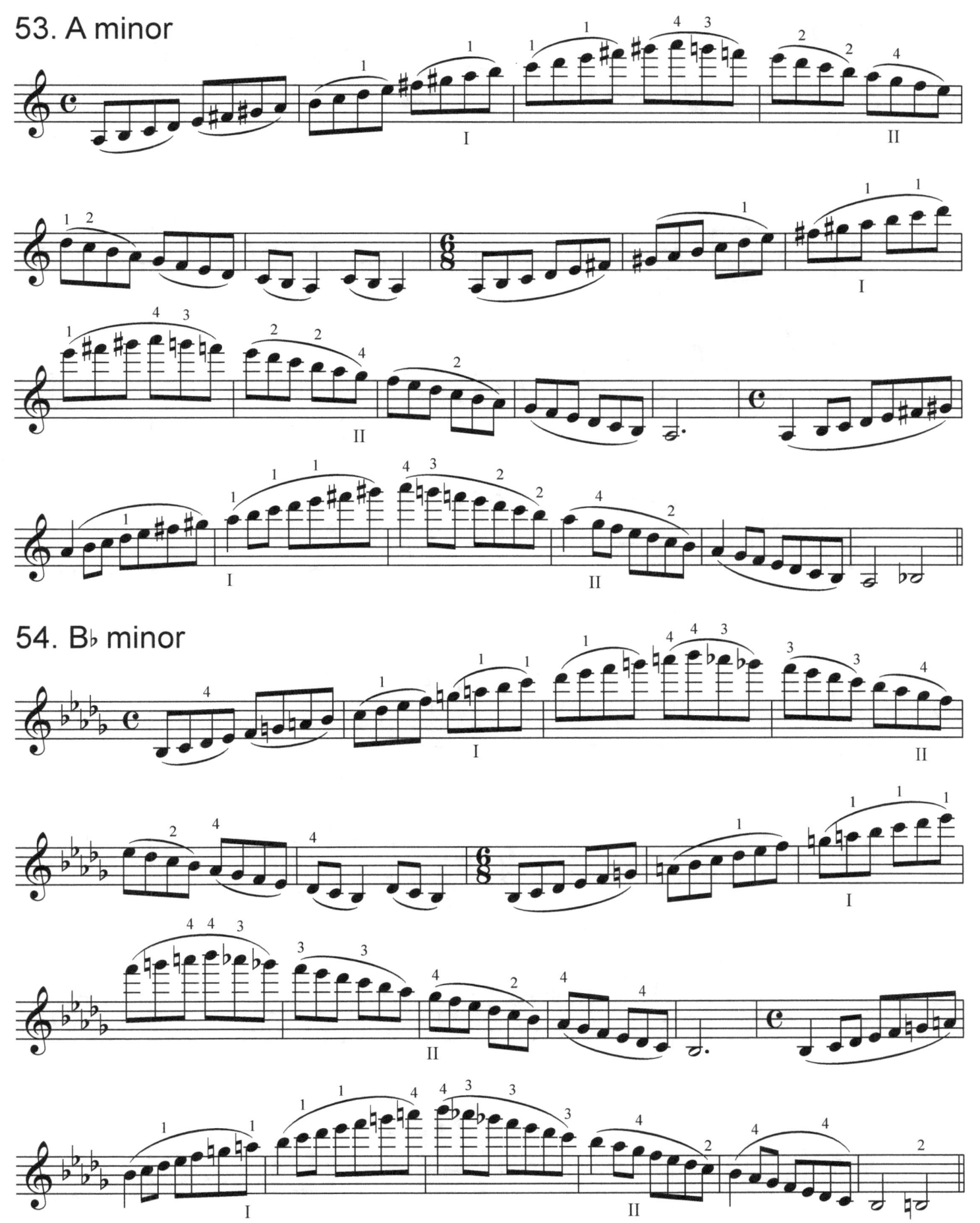

55. B minor

56. C minor

Three-Octave Scales for the Violin, Book One
Minor Scales for Speed
61

57. C# minor

58. D minor

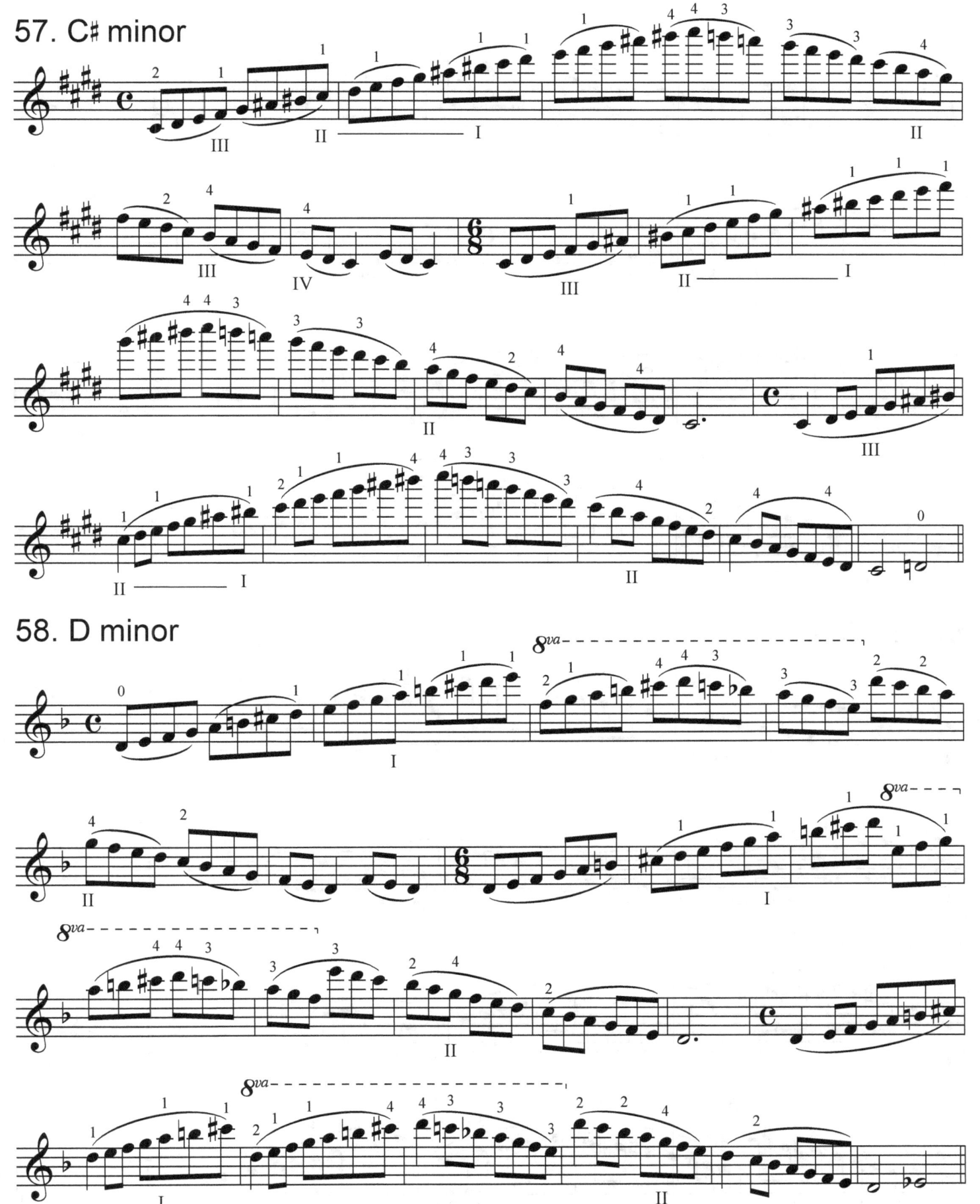

©2019 C. Harvey Publications All Rights Reserved.

Minor Scales for Speed

59. E♭ minor

60. E minor

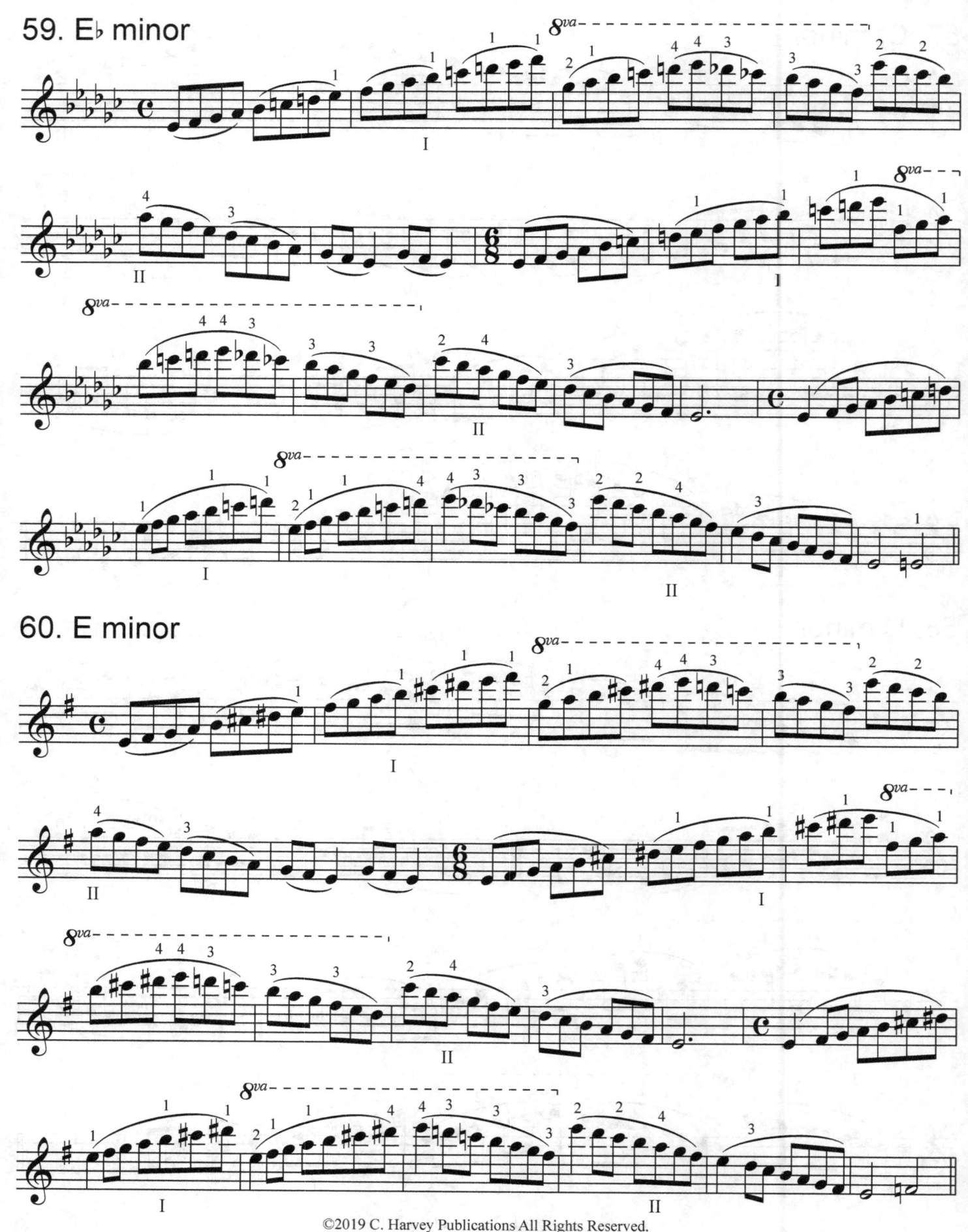

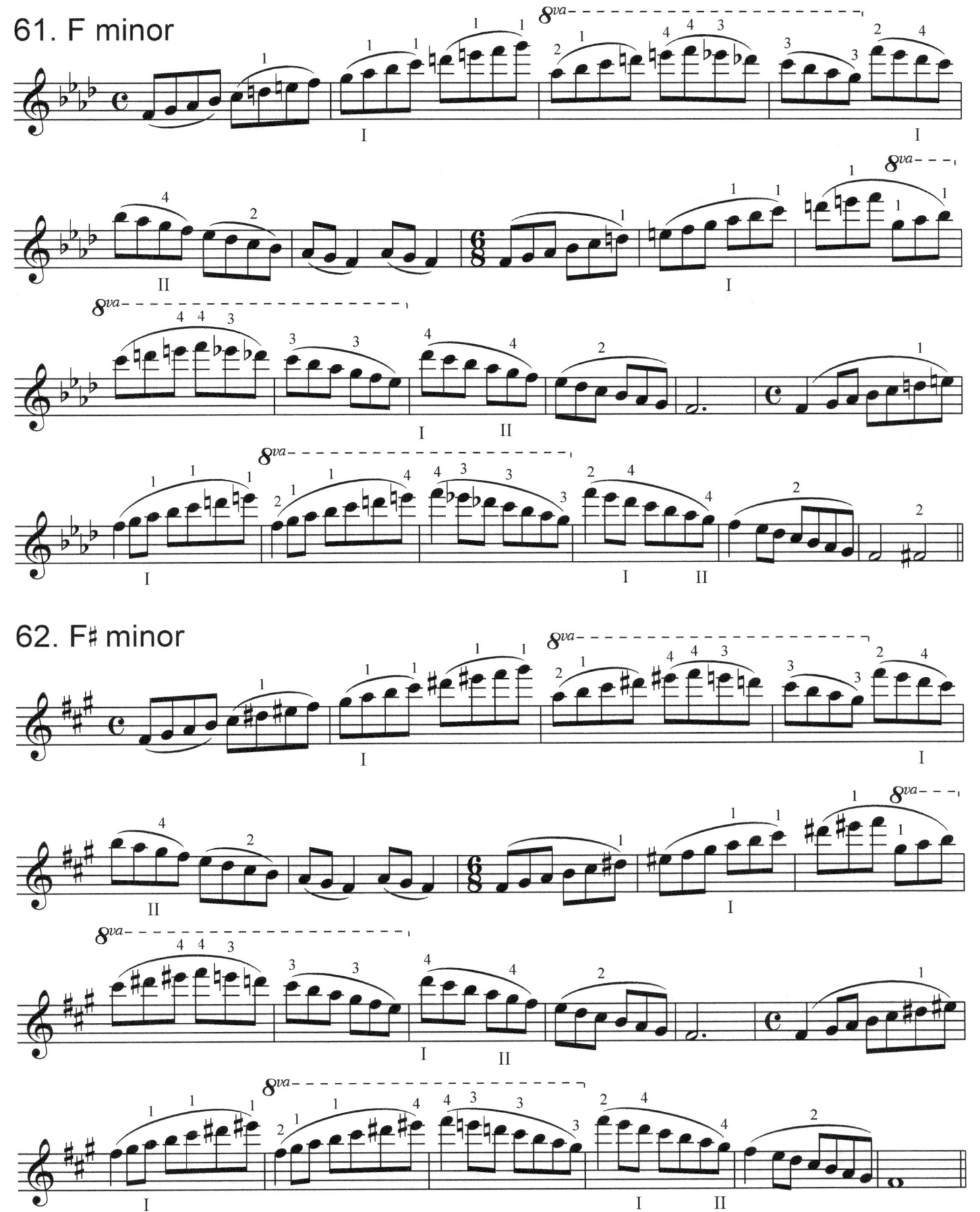

Part Six: Major Scales, Alternate Fingering

63. G major (alternate fingering) - Preparatory Shifting

64. G major (alternate fingering)

E minor is No. 96
G minor is No. 87

Scale with shifting guide notes

65. A♭ major (alt.) - Preparatory Shifting

67. A major (alt.) - Preparatory Shifting

Three-Octave Scales for the Violin, Book One Major Scales, Alternate Fingering 69

68. A major (alt.)

F# minor is No. 98
A minor is No. 89

Scale with shifting guide notes

©2019 C. Harvey Publications All Rights Reserved.

69. B♭ major (alt.) - Preparatory Shifting

Three-Octave Scales for the Violin, Book One   Major Scales, Alternate Fingering   71

70. B♭ major (alt.)

G minor is No. 87
B♭ minor is No. 90

©2019 C. Harvey Publications All Rights Reserved.

71. B major (alt.) - Preparatory Shifting

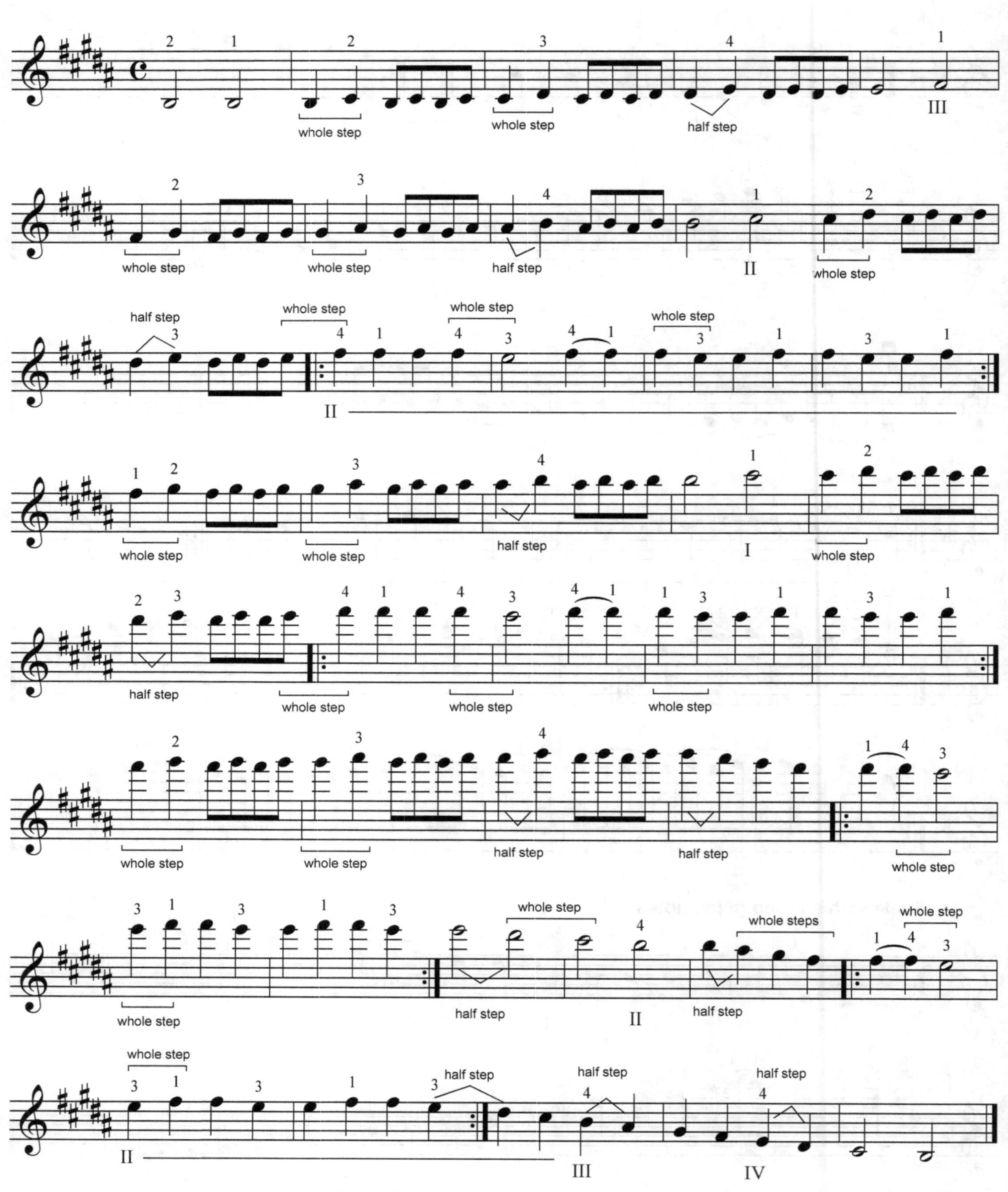

73. C major (alt.) - Preparatory Shifting

74. C major (alt.)

A minor is No. 89
C minor is No. 92

75. D♭ major (alt.) - Preparatory Shifting

77. D major (alt.) - Preparatory Shifting

Three-Octave Scales for the Violin, Book One Major Scales, Alternate Fingering 79

78. D major (alt.)

B minor is No. 91
D minor is No. 94

Scale with shifting guide notes

©2019 C. Harvey Publications All Rights Reserved.

79. E♭ major (alt.) - Preparatory Shifting

81. E major (alt.) - Preparatory Shifting

84 Major Scales, Alternate Fingering

83. F major (alt.) - Preparatory Shifting

85. F# major (alt.) - Preparatory Shifting

Part Seven: Minor Scales, Alternate Fingering

B♭ major is No. 70
G major is No. 64

87. G minor (alt.)

Three-Octave Scales for the Violin, Book One Minor Scales, Alternate Fingering 89

88. G♯ minor (alt.)

B major is No. 72
A♭ major is No. 66

©2019 C. Harvey Publications All Rights Reserved.

90 Minor Scales, Alternate Fingering
Three-Octave Scales for the Violin, Book One

89. A minor (alt.)

C major is No. 74
A major is No. 68

©2019 C. Harvey Publications All Rights Reserved.

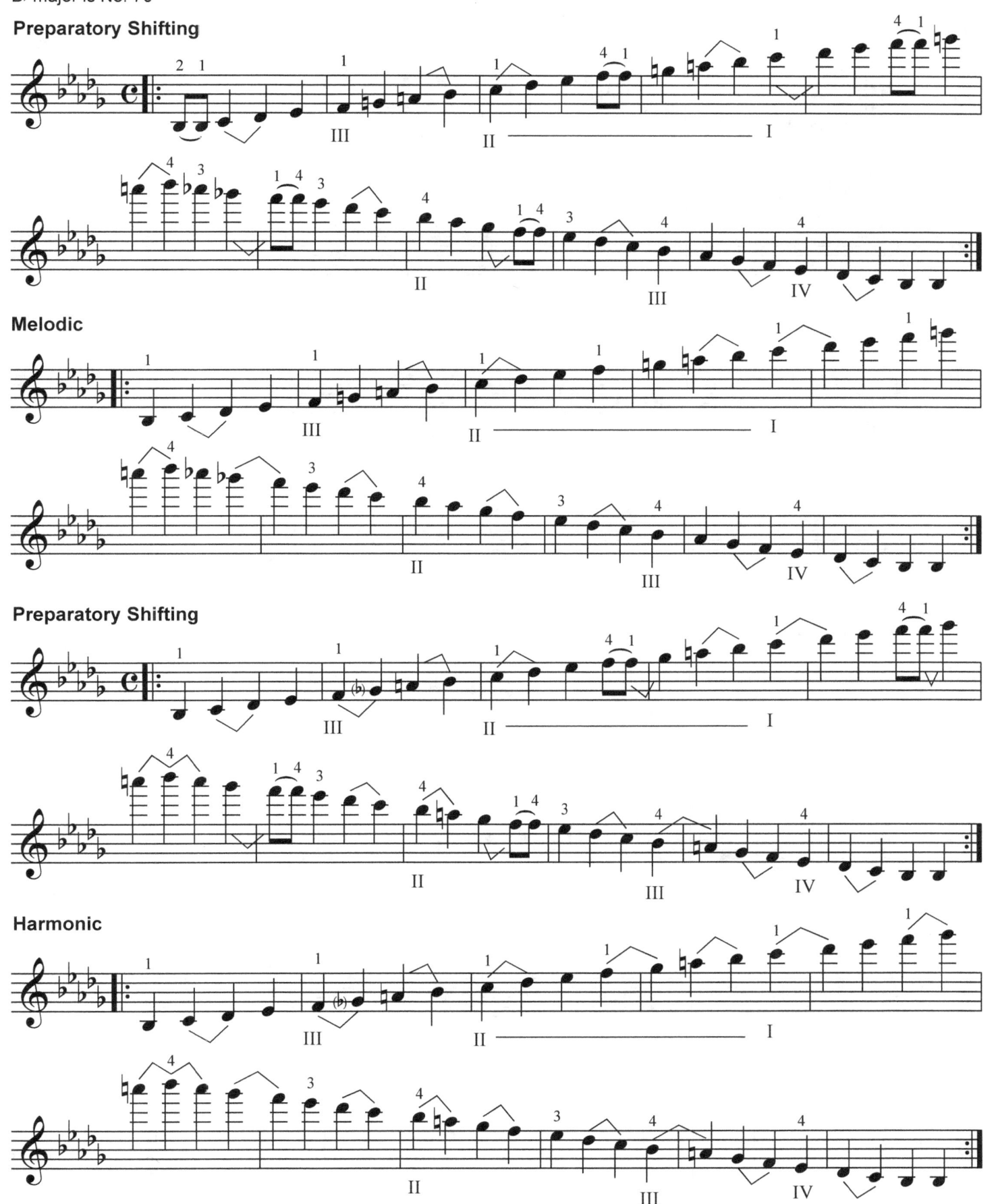

92 Minor Scales, Alternate Fingering — Three-Octave Scales for the Violin, Book One

D major is No. 78
B major is No. 72

91. B minor (alt.)

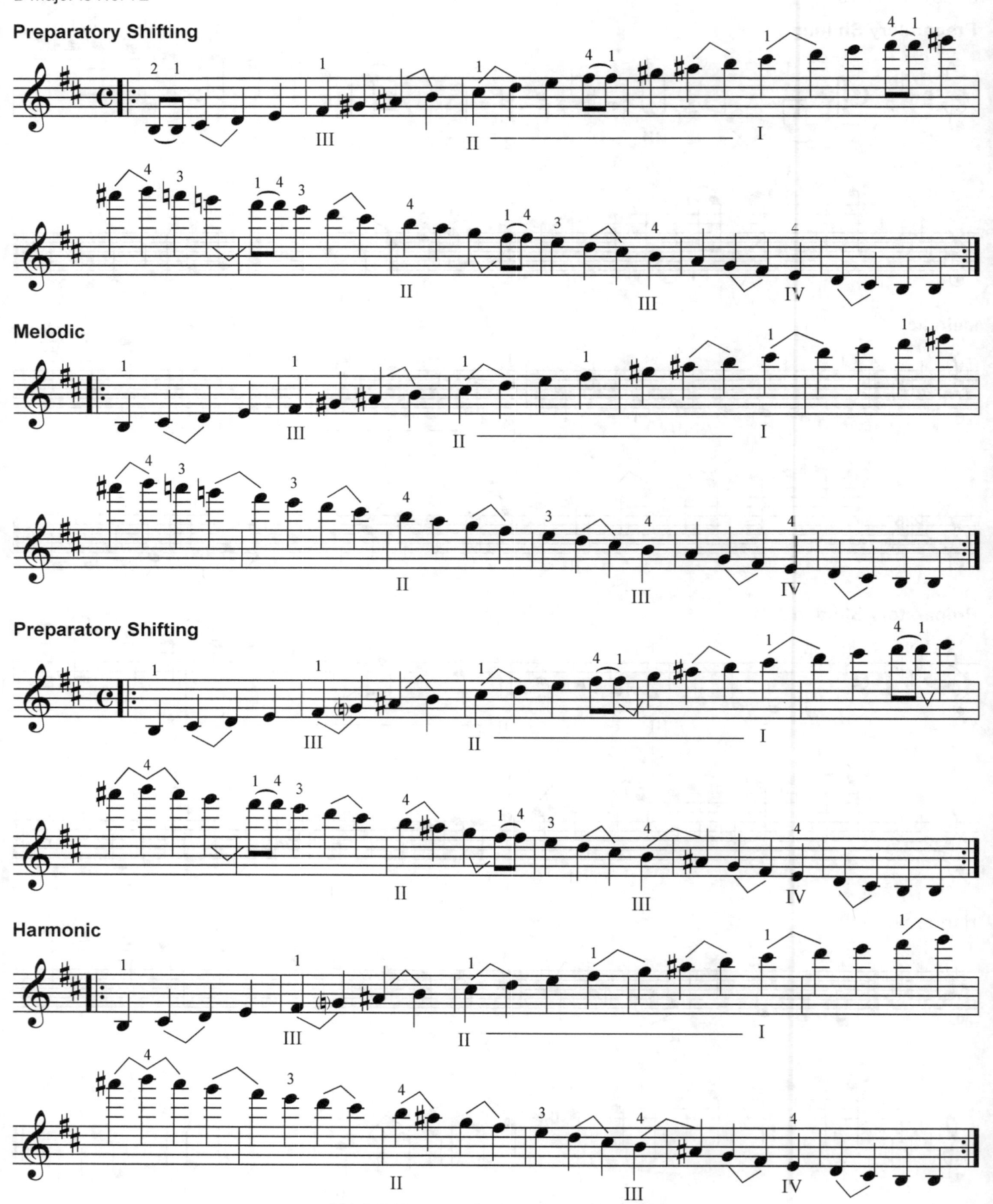

©2019 C. Harvey Publications All Rights Reserved.

92. C minor (alt.)

Eb major is No. 80
C major is No. 74

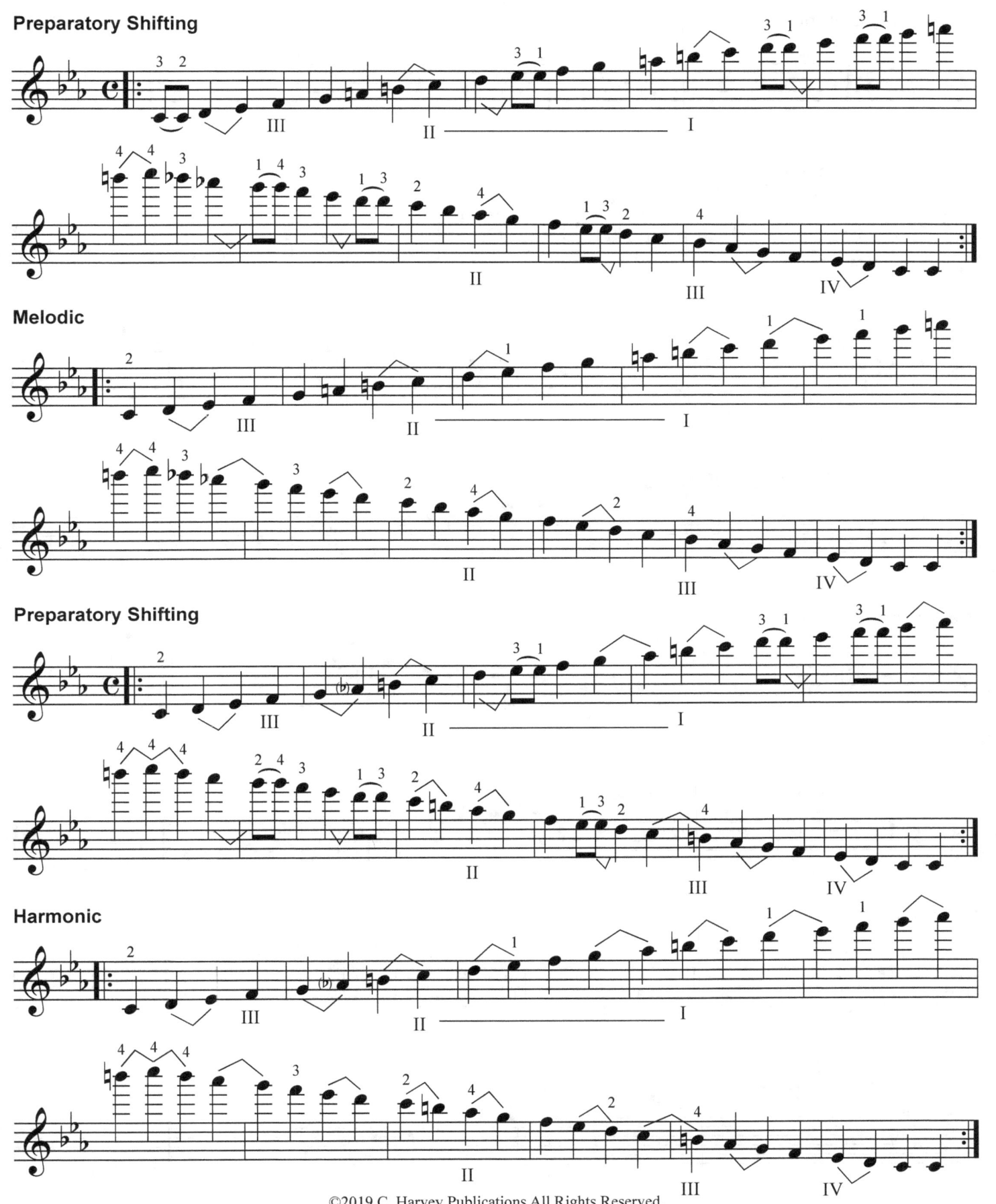

93. C# minor (alt.)

Minor Scales, Alternate Fingering

E major is No. 82
C# major is No. 76

Preparatory Shifting

Melodic

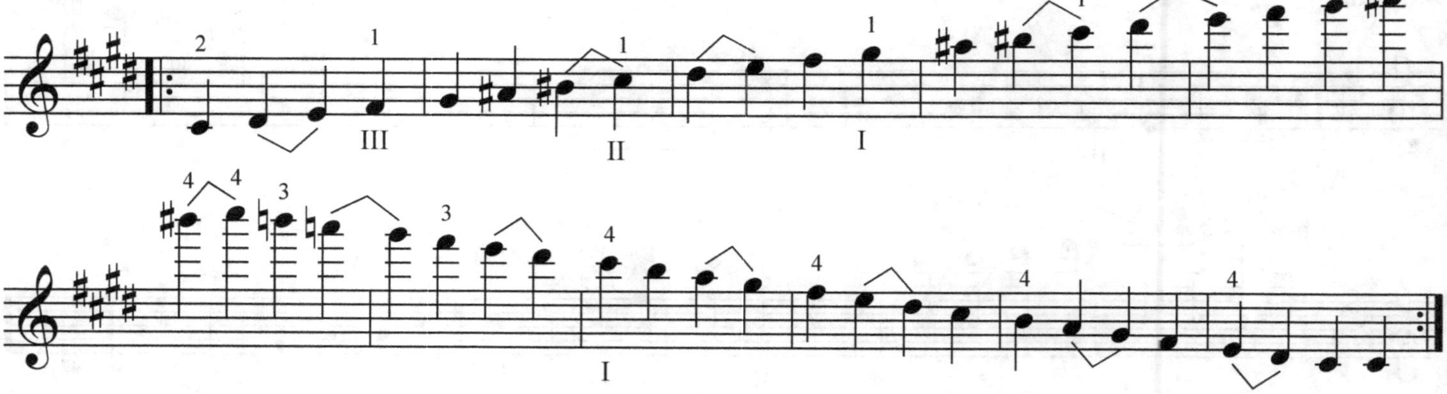

Preparatory Shifting

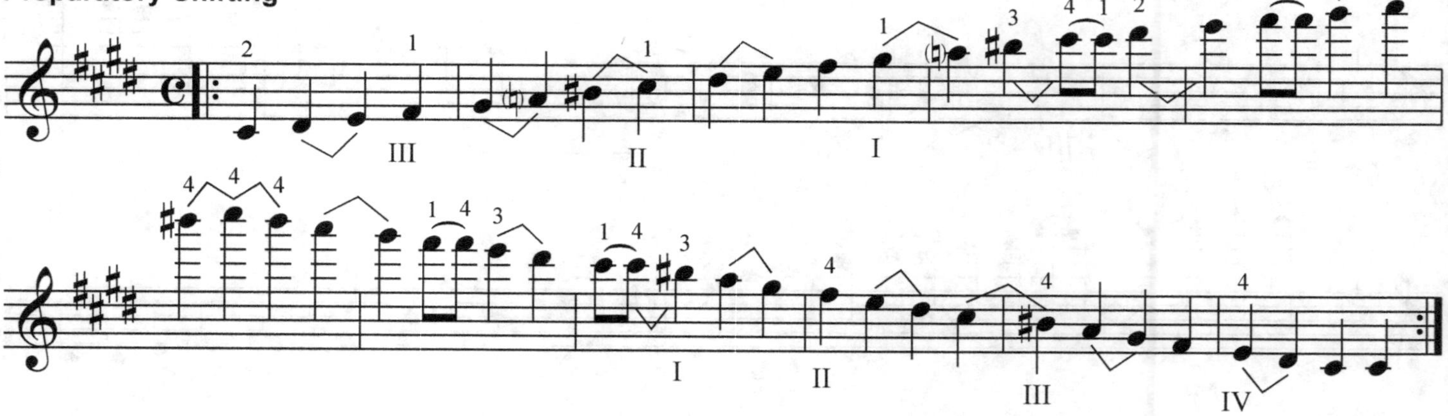

Harmonic

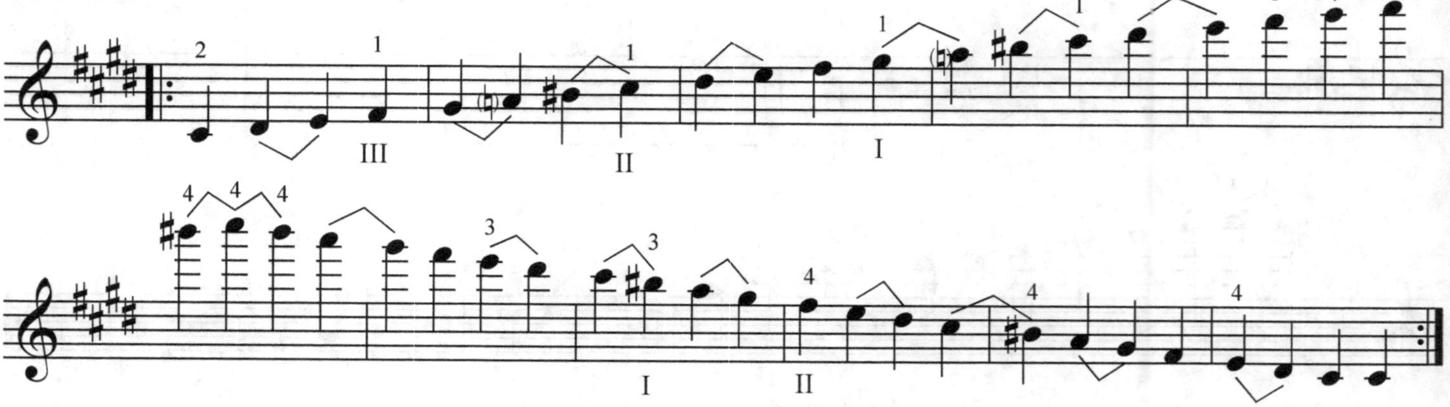

98 Minor Scales, Alternate Fingering

A♭ major is No. 66
F major is No. 84

97. F minor (alt.)

Preparatory Shifting

Melodic

Preparatory Shifting

Harmonic

©2019 C. Harvey Publications All Rights Reserved.

Part Eight: Chromatic Scale with Alternate Fingering

99. Chromatic Scale Shifting (alt.)

100. Chromatic Scale Slur Patterns (alt.)

A Universal Fingering

On the violin, **most scales can be played with just one fingering**. This can be useful if you are trying to memorize the scales in a hurry or if you want to work on learning the same spacing in all of the different positions.

Because this fingering starts on a first finger, G major and G minor scales are omitted. If you are only learning scales with the universal fingering, you could use pages 8, 9, and 32 to learn these scales.

The exercises in the next section work on shifting and playing across strings. At the end of each key, move your hand up 1/2 step and continue the exercise in the next key. Be very precise when starting each key so that you do not play the rest of the scale out of tune. Check your notes with open strings whenever possible to ensure you have shifted correctly.

When the complete scales are listed, starting on page 122, **optional shifting measures are included at the end of each scale to help you find the first note of the next scale.** These measures are most helpful if you are preparing to play the scales out of order (for instance, in an audition.)

Here is an overview of the universal fingering:

G string   D string   A string   E string
1 2 3 4 1 2 3 4 1 2 1 2 3 4 1 2 1 2 1 2 3 4

And coming back down the scale:
E string   A string   D string   G string
(4) 3 2 1 2 1 2 1 4 3 2 1 2 1 4 3 2 1 4 3 2 1

Three-Octave Scales for the Violin, BOOK ONE   103

Part Nine: Exercises for Universal Fingering

Exercise No. 1 for Universal Fingering

Note: All patterns start on the G string.

©2019 C. Harvey Publications All Rights Reserved.

Exercise No. 2 for Universal Fingering

Three-Octave Scales for the Violin, Book One
Exercises, Universal Fingering — 105

©2019 C. Harvey Publications All Rights Reserved.

Exercise No. 3 for Universal Fingering

Three-Octave Scales for the Violin, Book One — Exercises, Universal Fingering 107

Exercise No. 4 for Universal Fingering

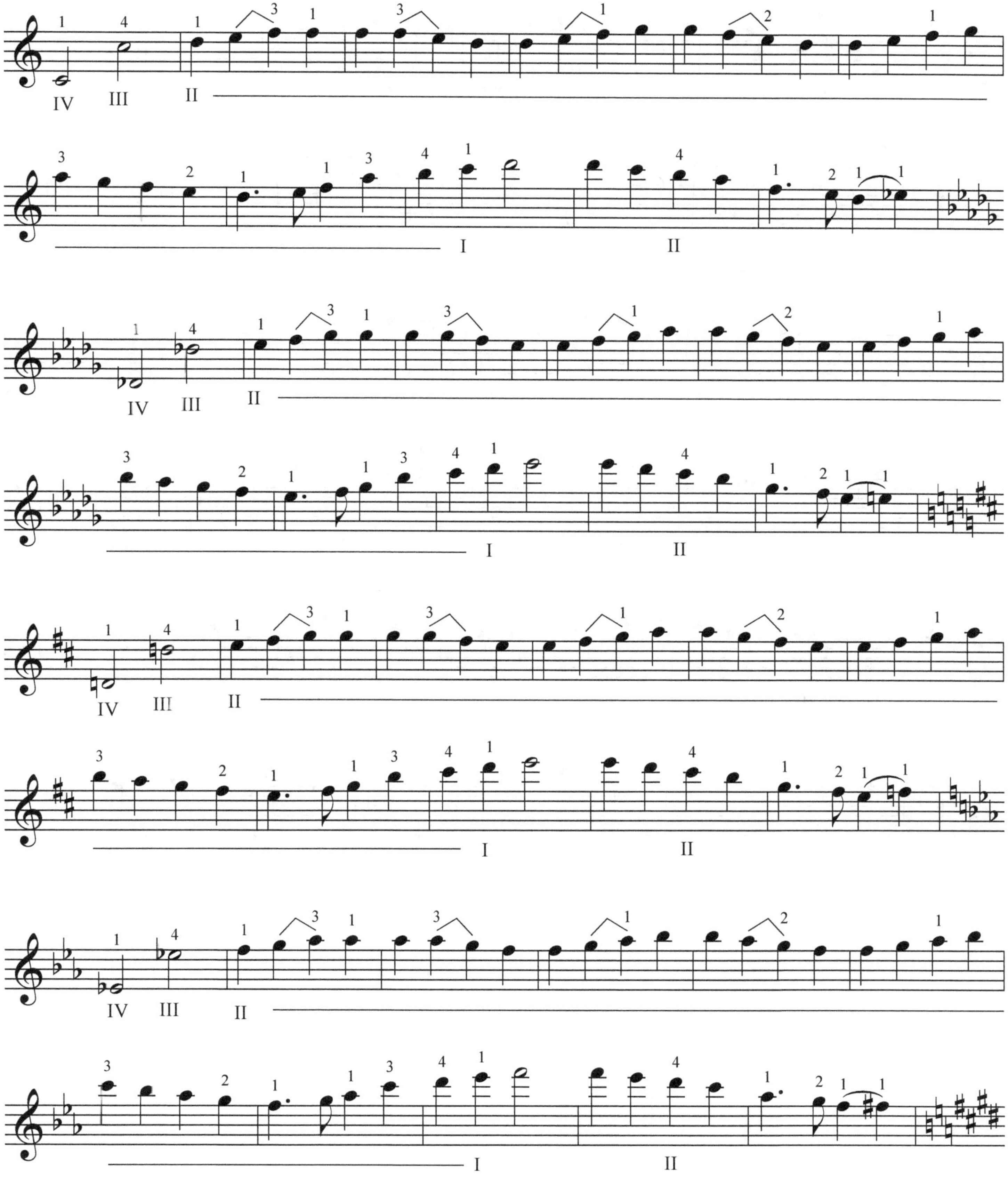

Three-Octave Scales for the Violin, Book One

Exercises, Universal Fingering 109

110 Exercises, Universal Fingering — Three-Octave Scales for the Violin, Book One

Exercise No. 5 for Universal Fingering

Exercise No. 6 for Universal Fingering

Three-Octave Scales for the Violin, Book One — Exercises, Universal Fingering 113

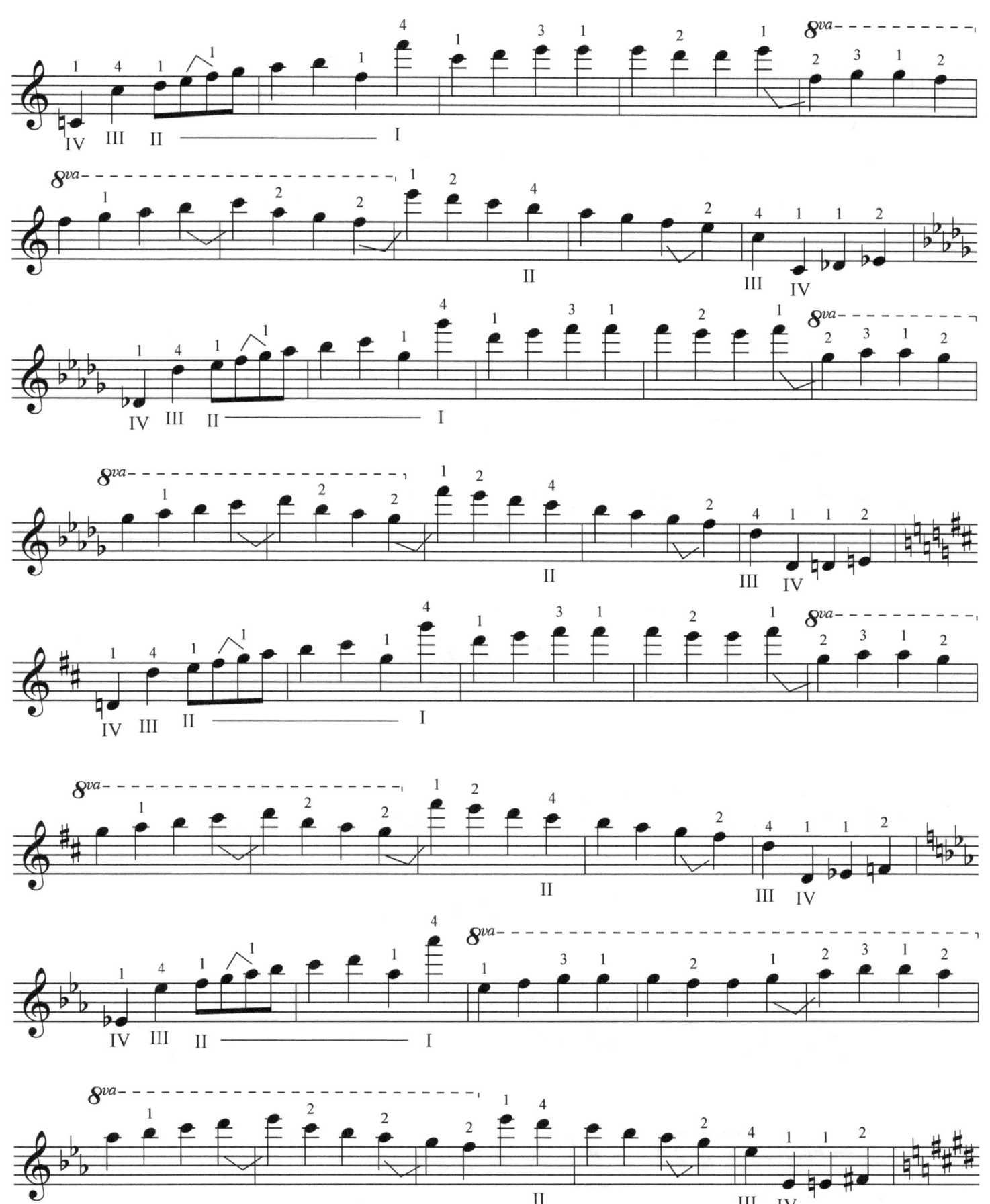

©2019 C. Harvey Publications All Rights Reserved.

114 Exercises, Universal Fingering

Exercise No. 7 for Universal Fingering

Three-Octave Scales for the Violin, Book One
Exercises, Universal Fingering 115

©2019 C. Harvey Publications All Rights Reserved.

Exercise No. 8 for Universal Fingering

Three-Octave Scales for the Violin, Book One

Exercises, Universal Fingering 117

Exercise No. 9 for Universal Fingering

Three-Octave Scales for the Violin, Book One Exercises, Universal Fingering

120 Exercises, Universal Fingering   Three-Octave Scales for the Violin, Book One

©2019 C. Harvey Publications All Rights Reserved.

Part Ten: Major Scales with Universal Fingering

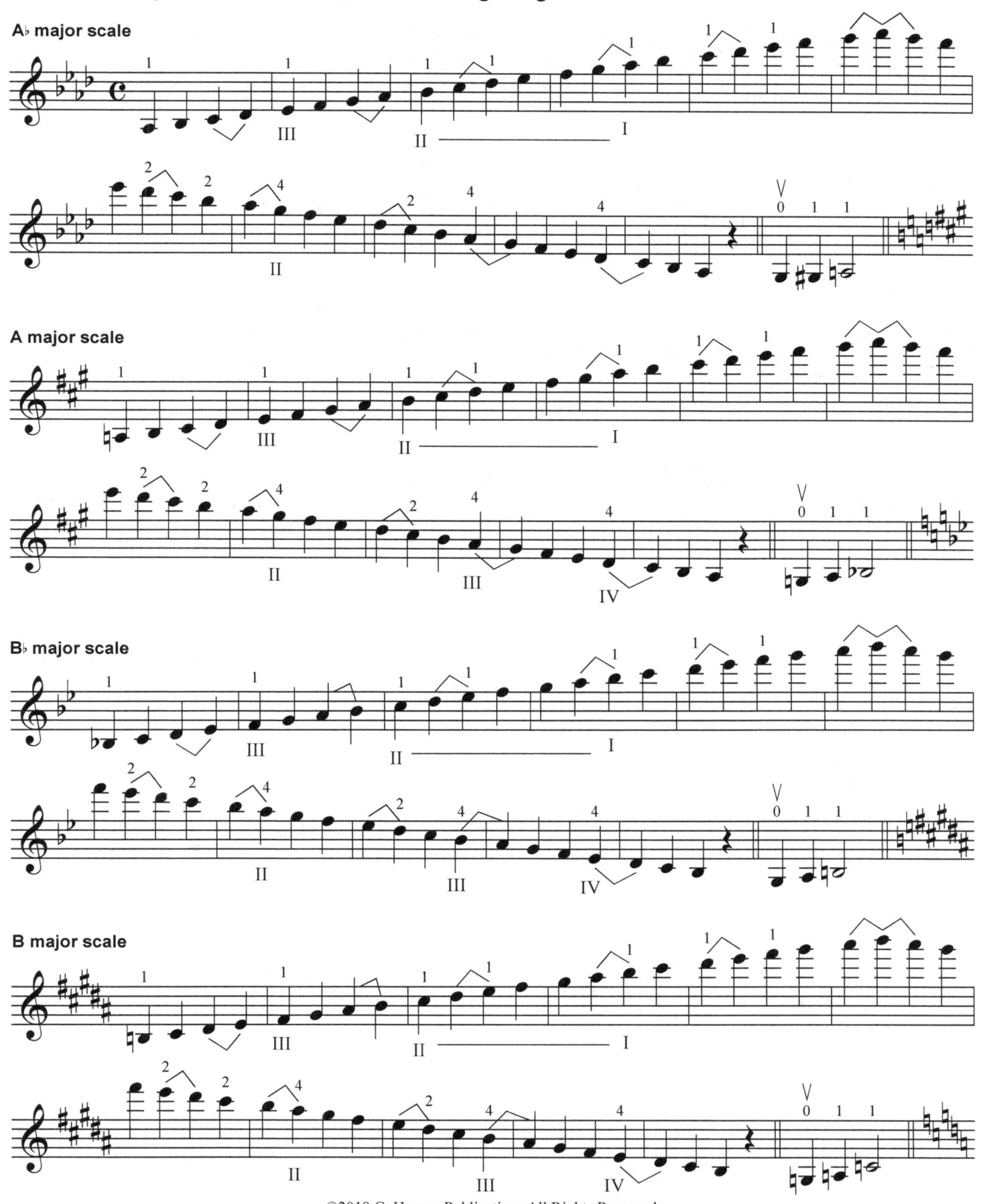

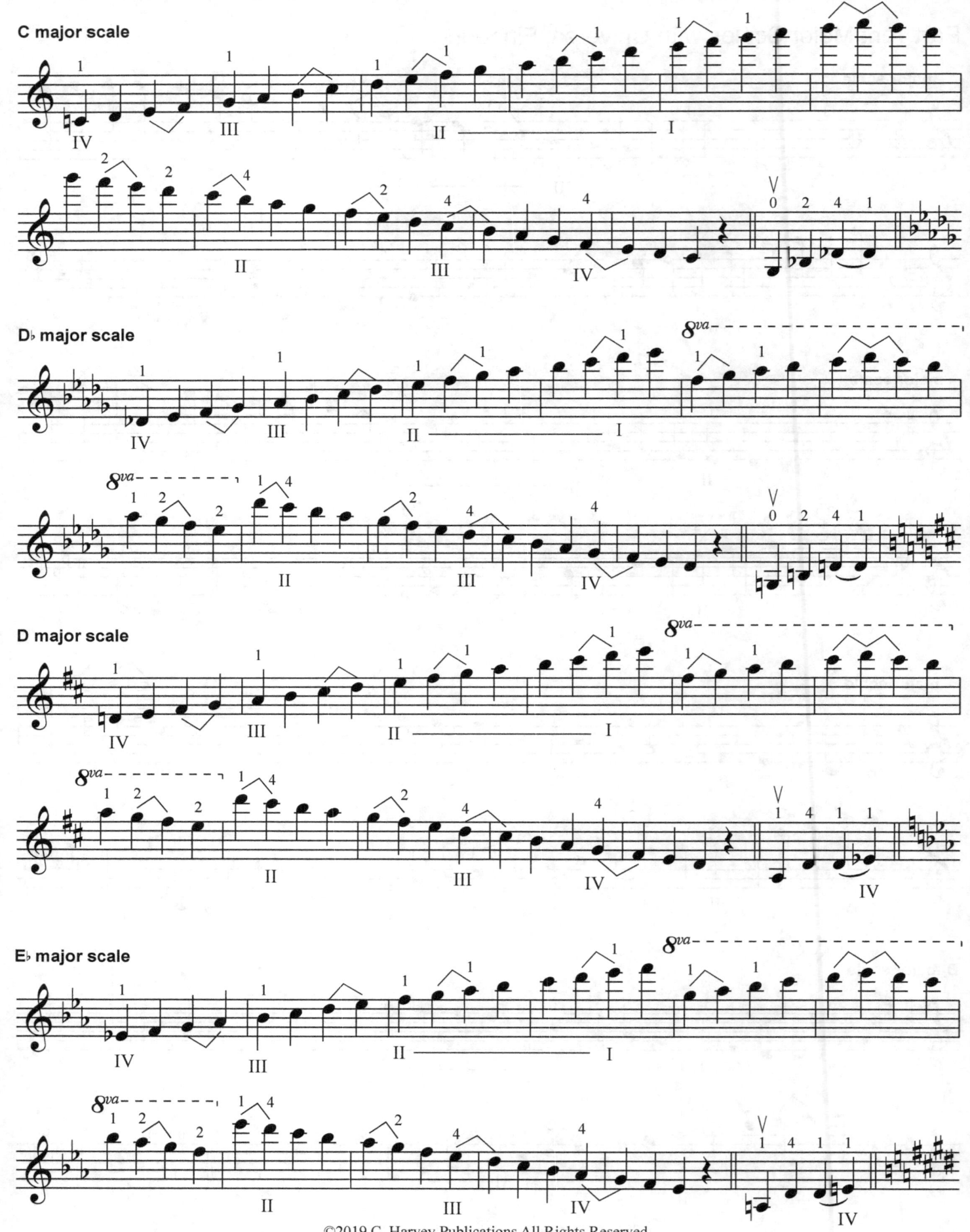

Three-Octave Scales for the Violin, Book One   Major Scales, Universal Fingering 123

E major scale

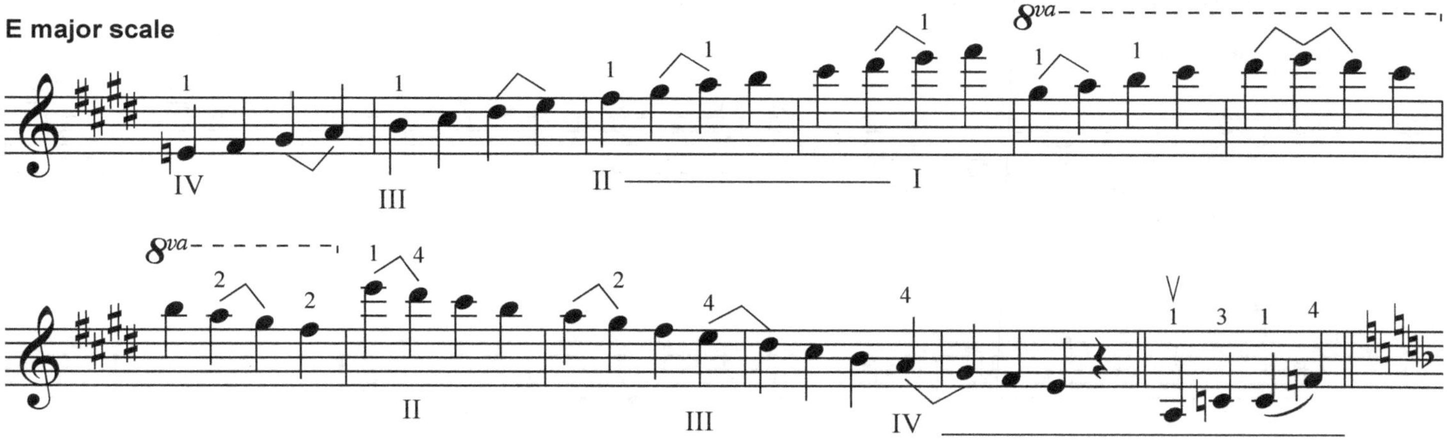

F major scale

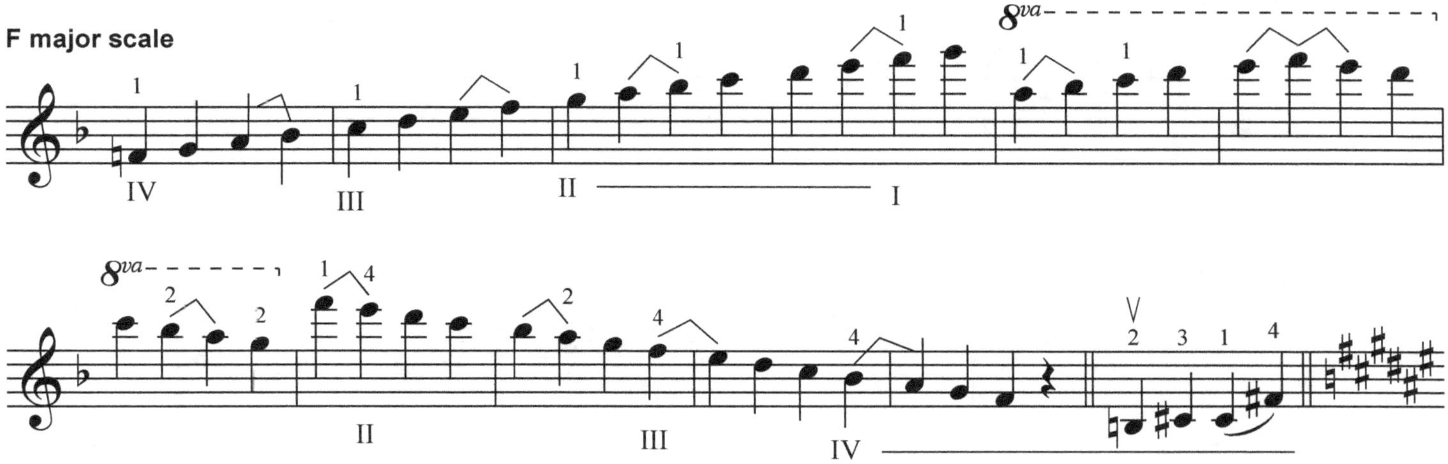

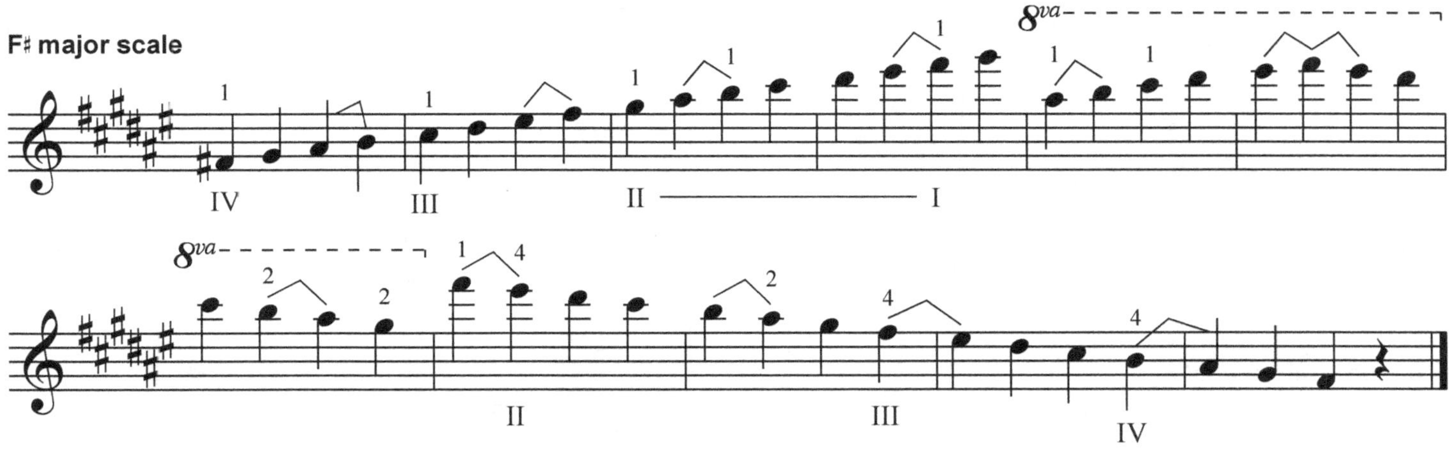

F# major scale

©2019 C. Harvey Publications All Rights Reserved.

Part Eleven: Melodic Minor Scales with Universal Fingering

G♯ melodic minor scale

A melodic minor scale

B♭ melodic minor scale

B melodic minor scale

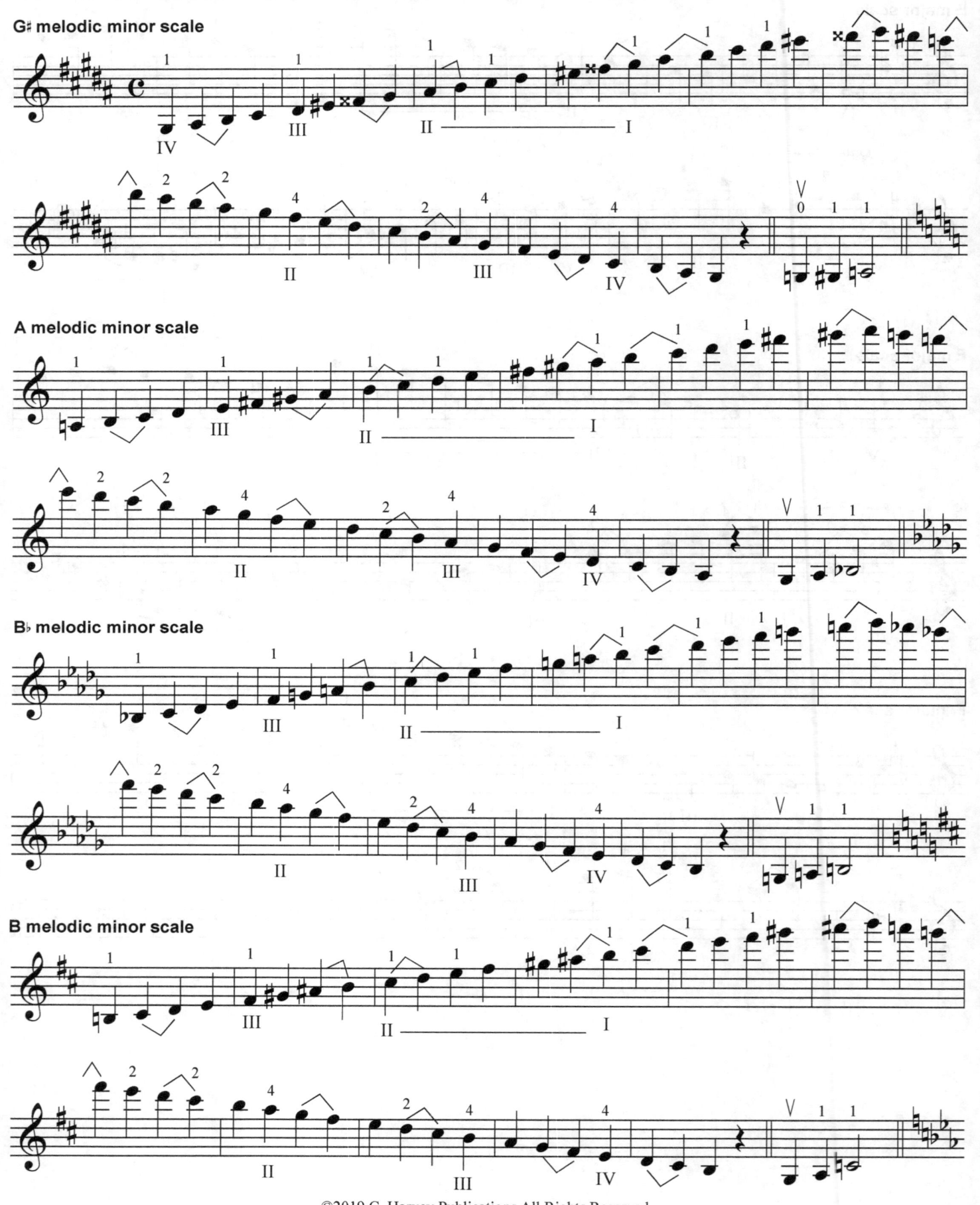

©2019 C. Harvey Publications All Rights Reserved.

Three-Octave Scales for the Violin, Book One Melodic Minor Scales, Universal Fingering 125

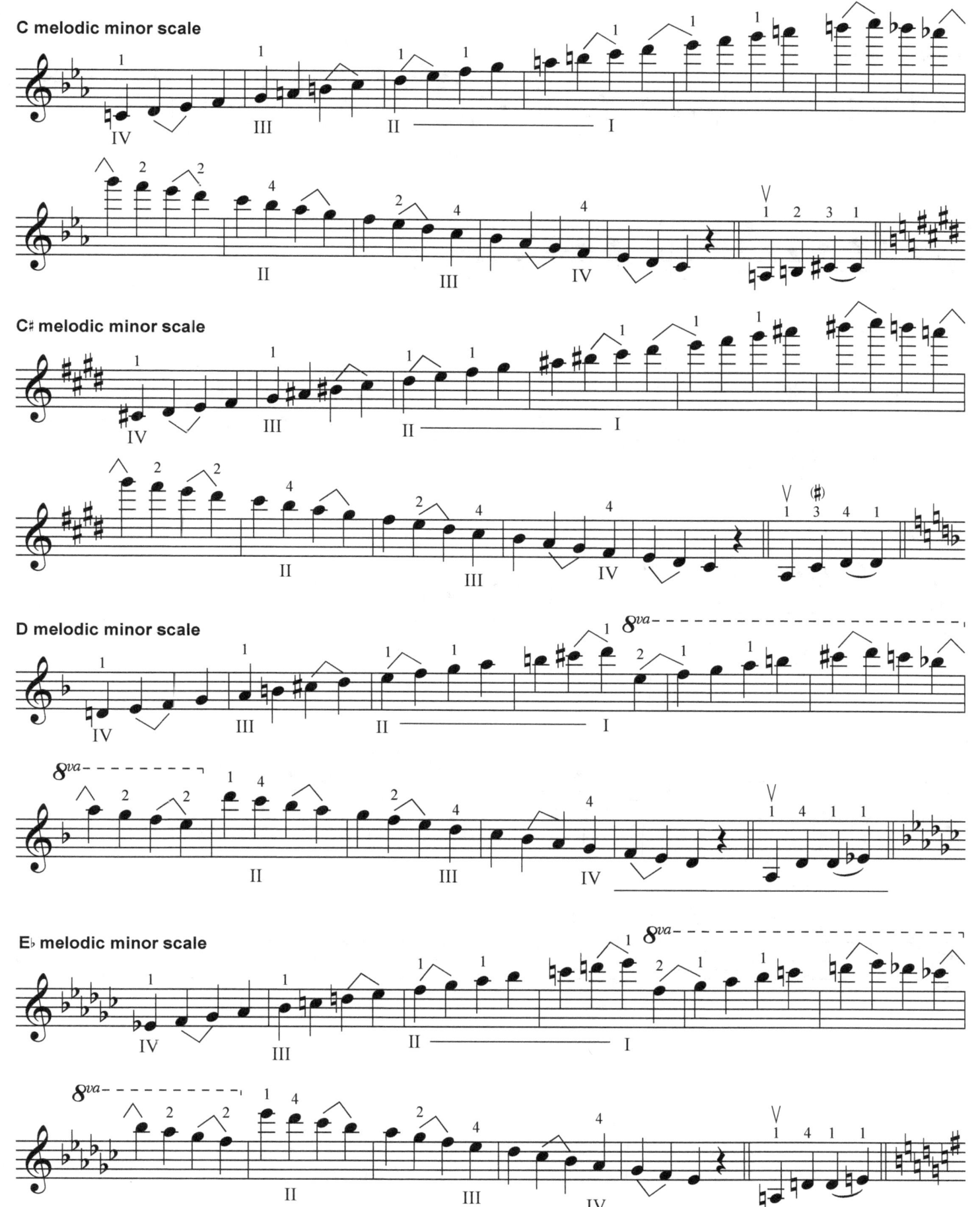

126 Melodic Minor Scales, Universal Fingering

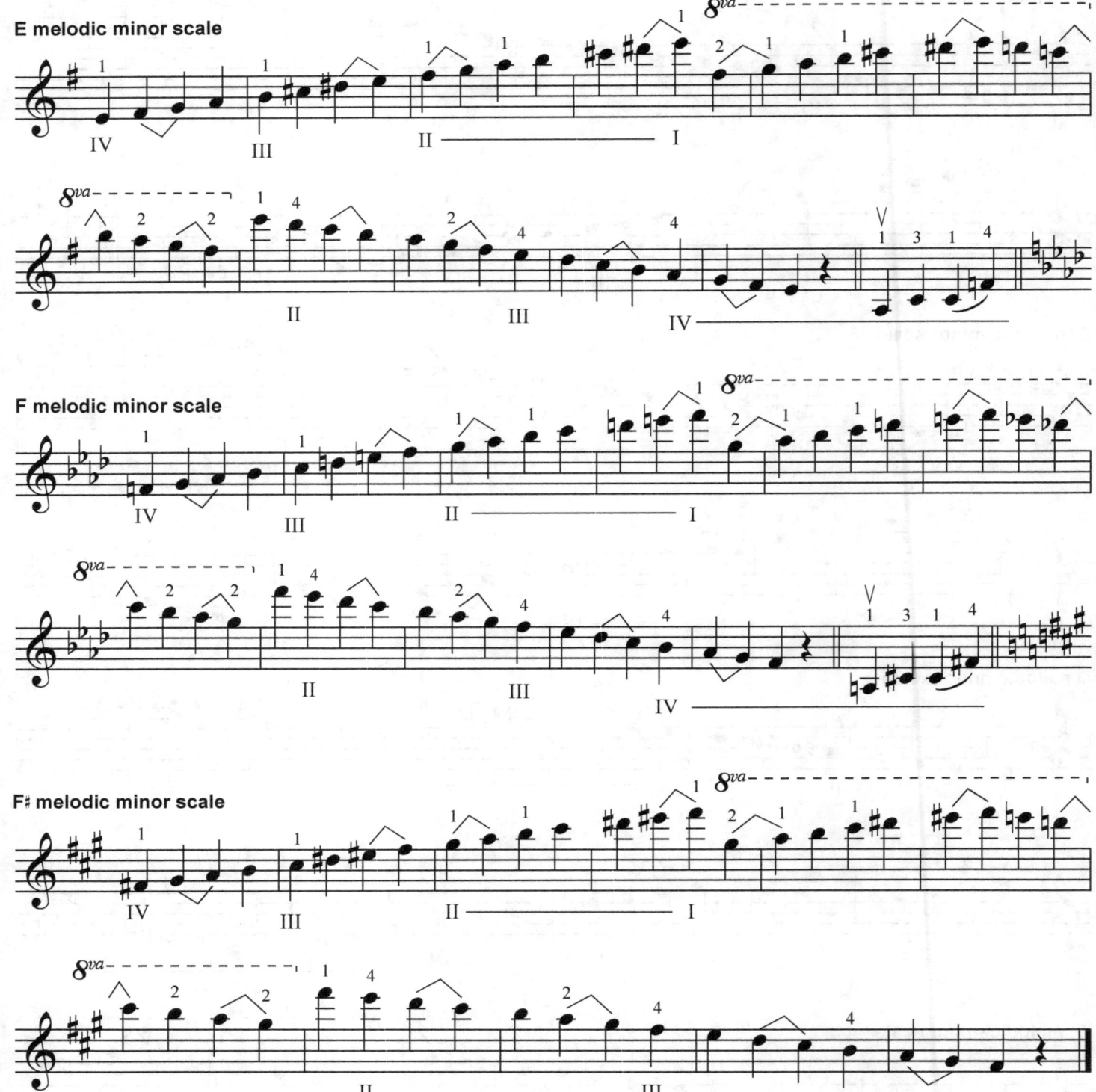

Part Twelve: Harmonic Minor Scales with Universal Fingering

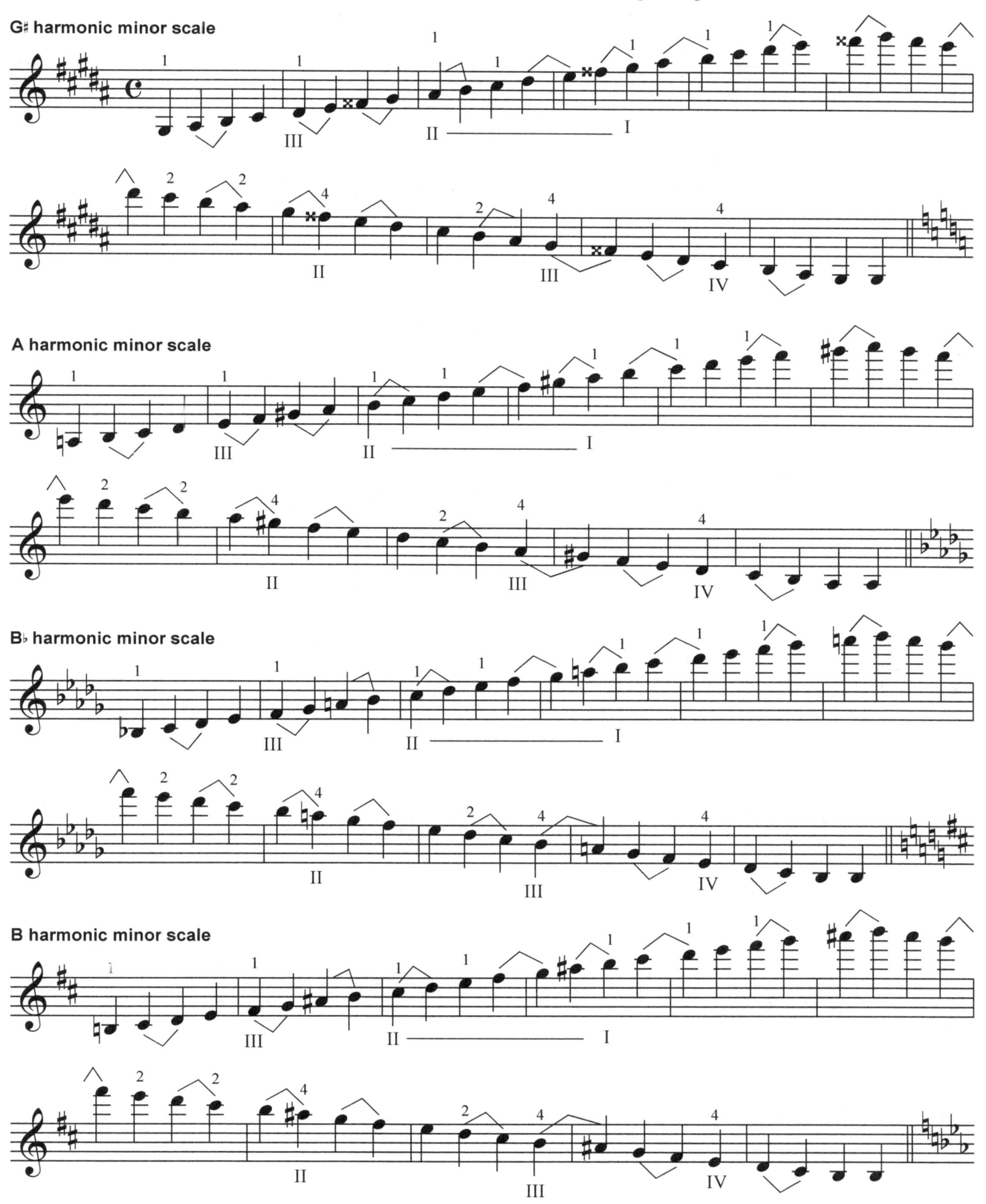

128 Harmonic Minor Scales, Universal Fingering — Three-Octave Scales for the Violin, Book One

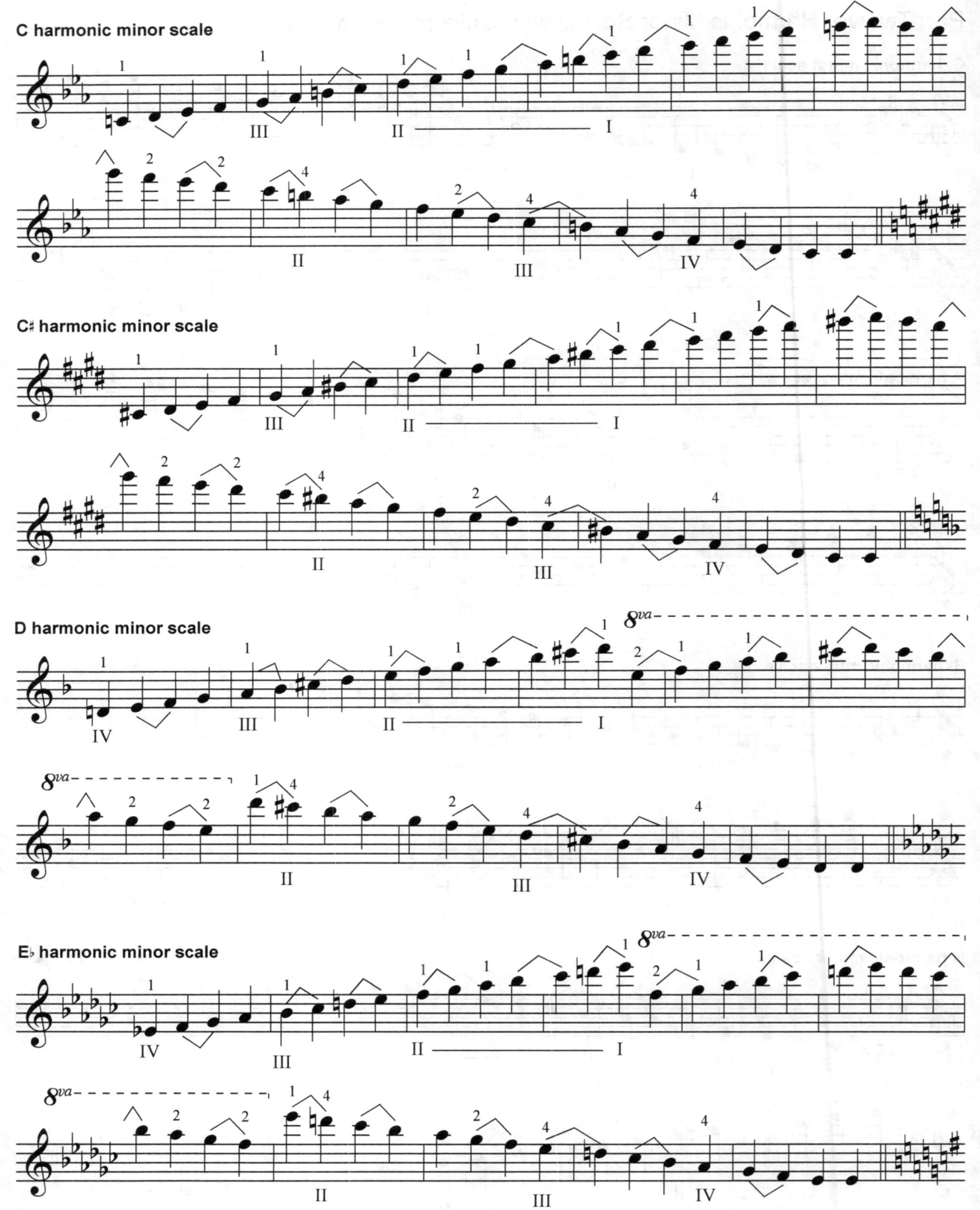

©2019 C. Harvey Publications All Rights Reserved.

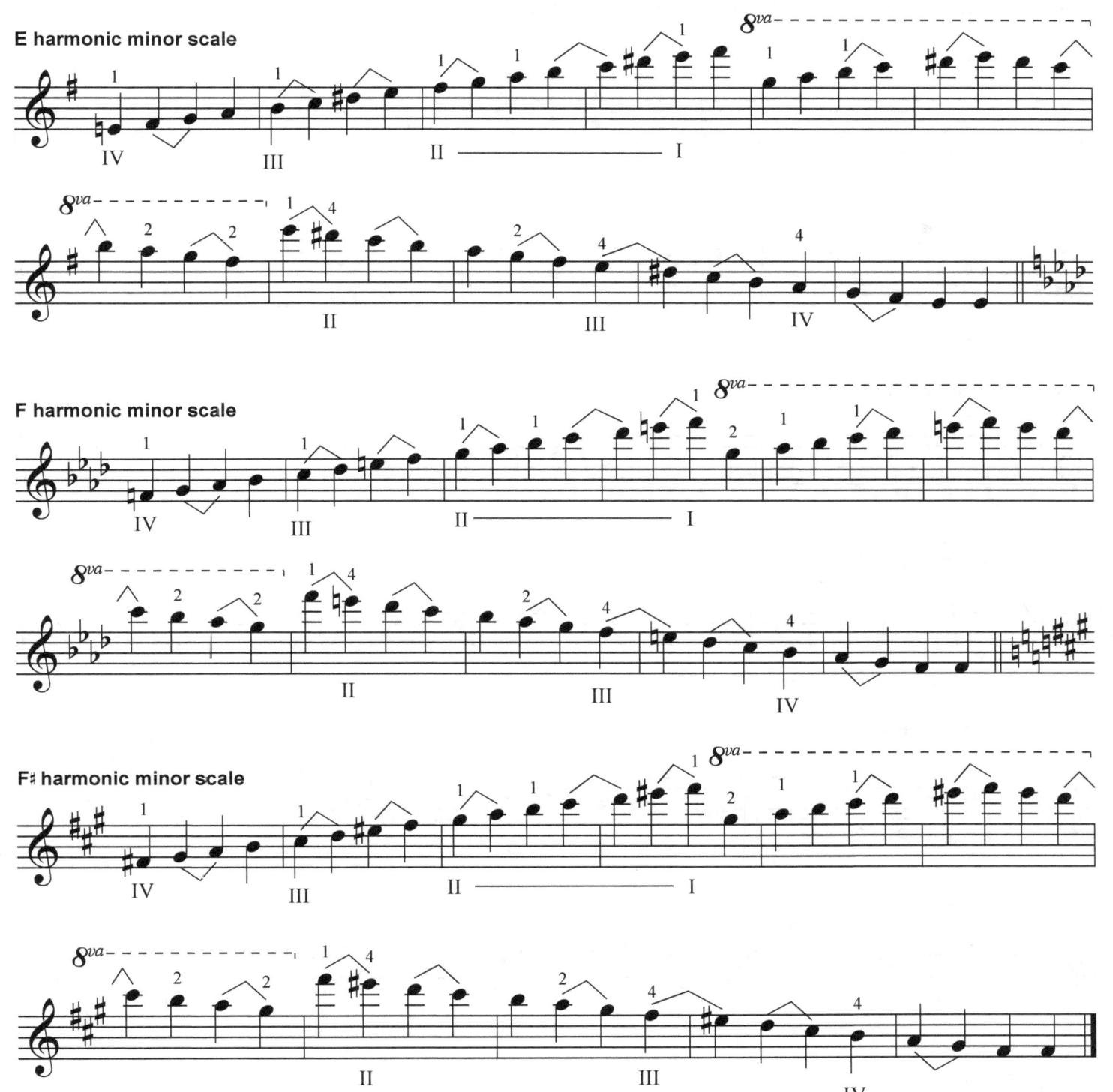

Part Thirteen: Complete Scales, Main Fingering

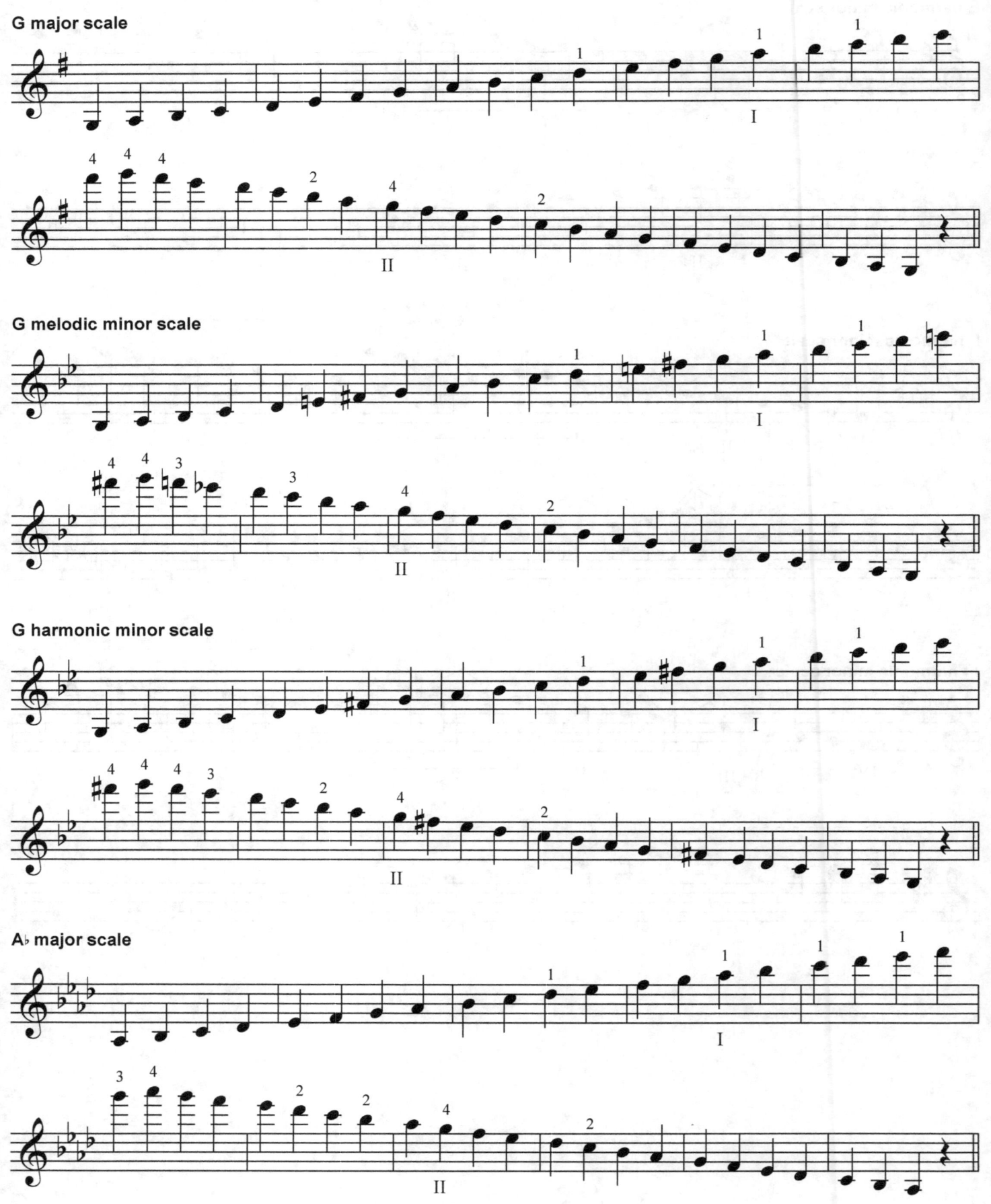

Three-Octave Scales for the Violin, Book One — Complete Scales, Main Fingering — 131

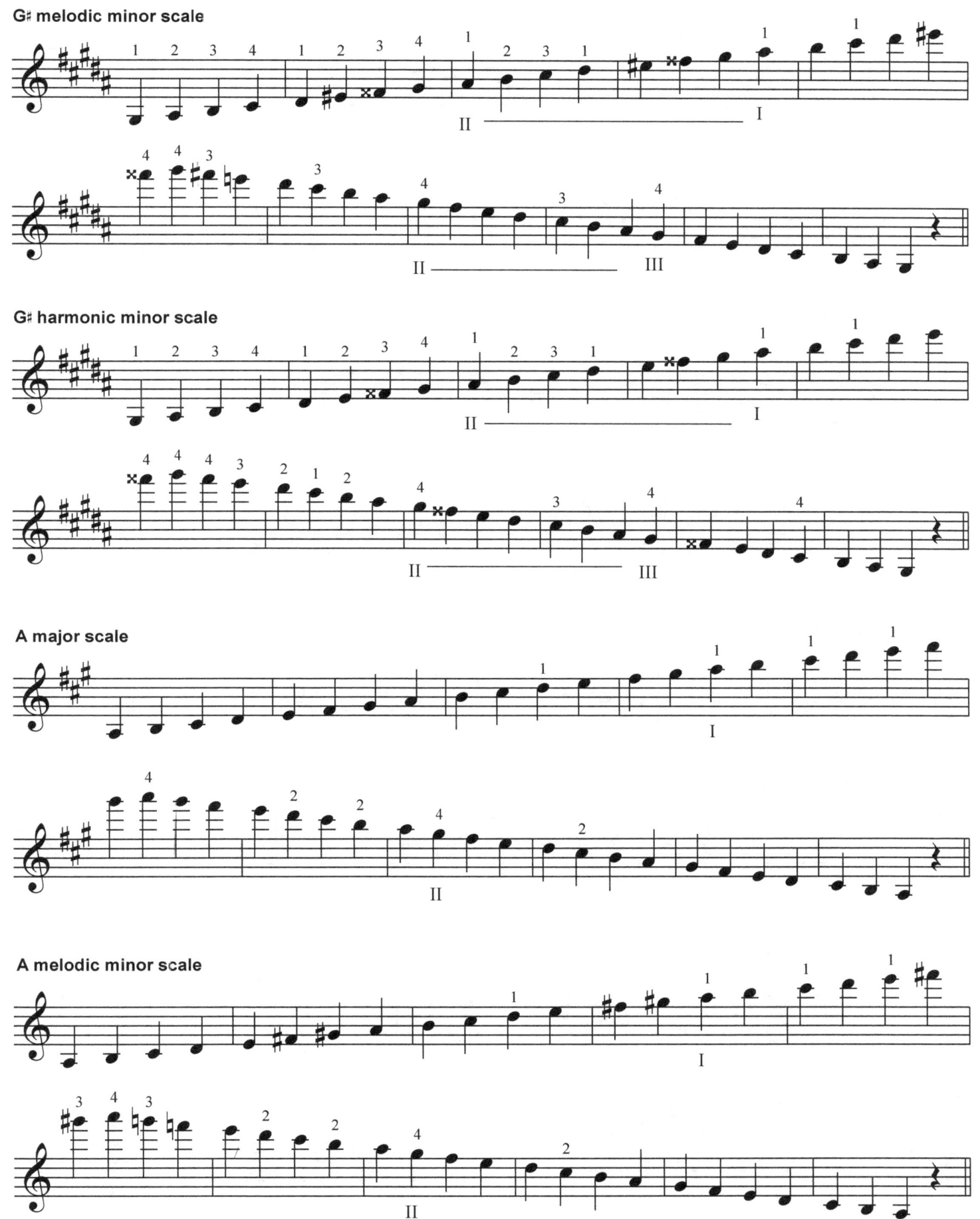

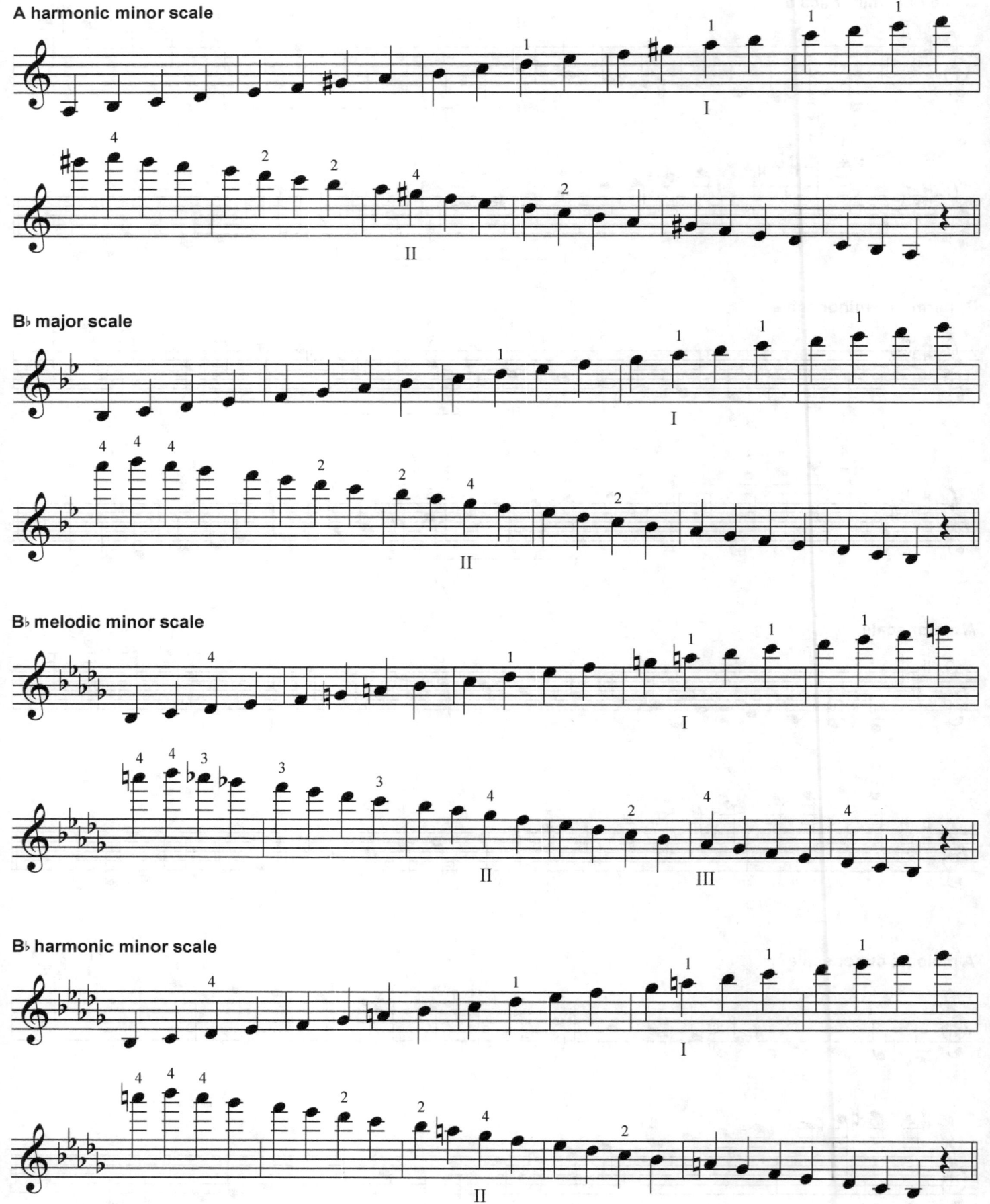

Three-Octave Scales for the Violin, Book One Complete Scales, Main Fingering 133

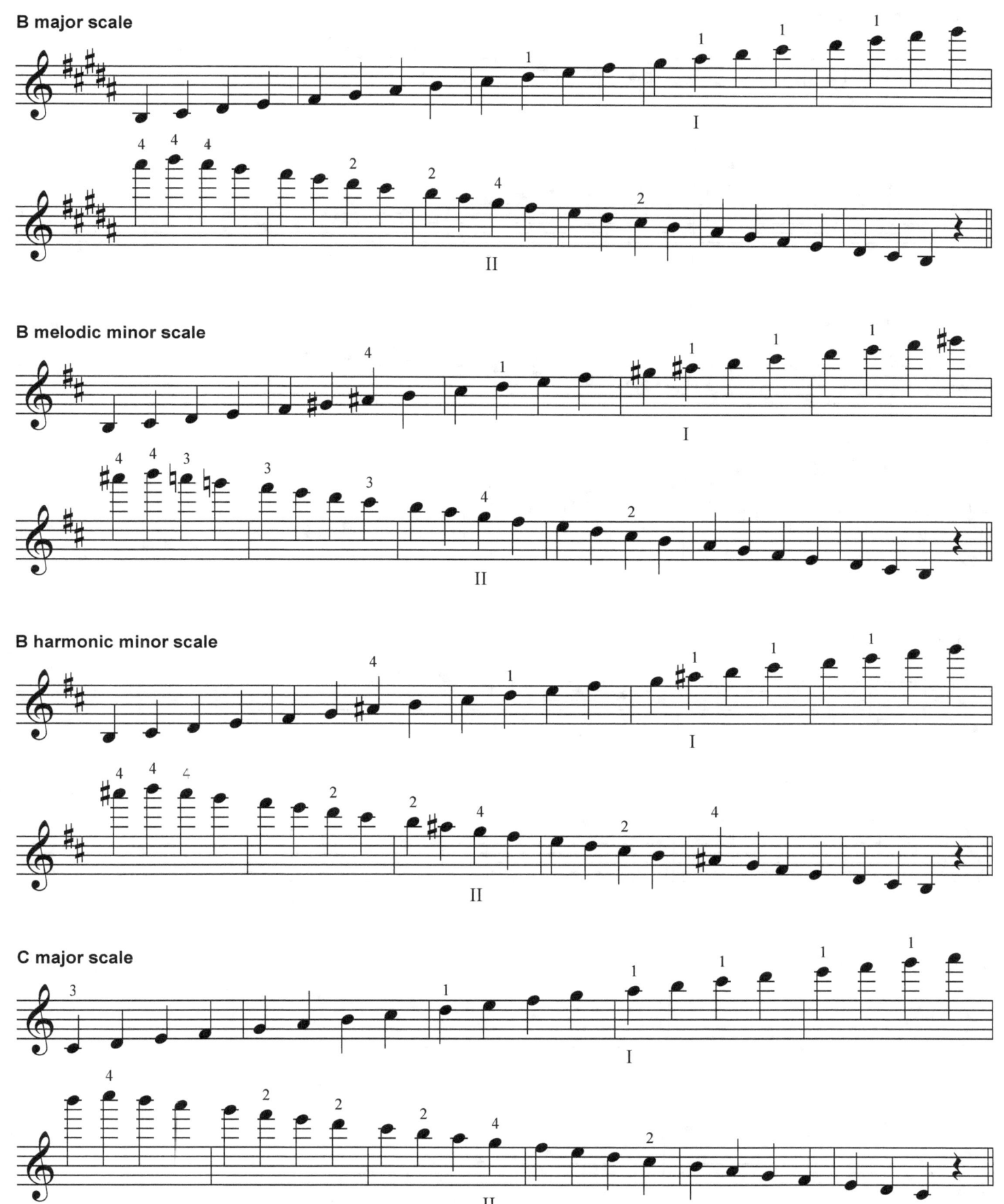

©2019 C. Harvey Publications All Rights Reserved.

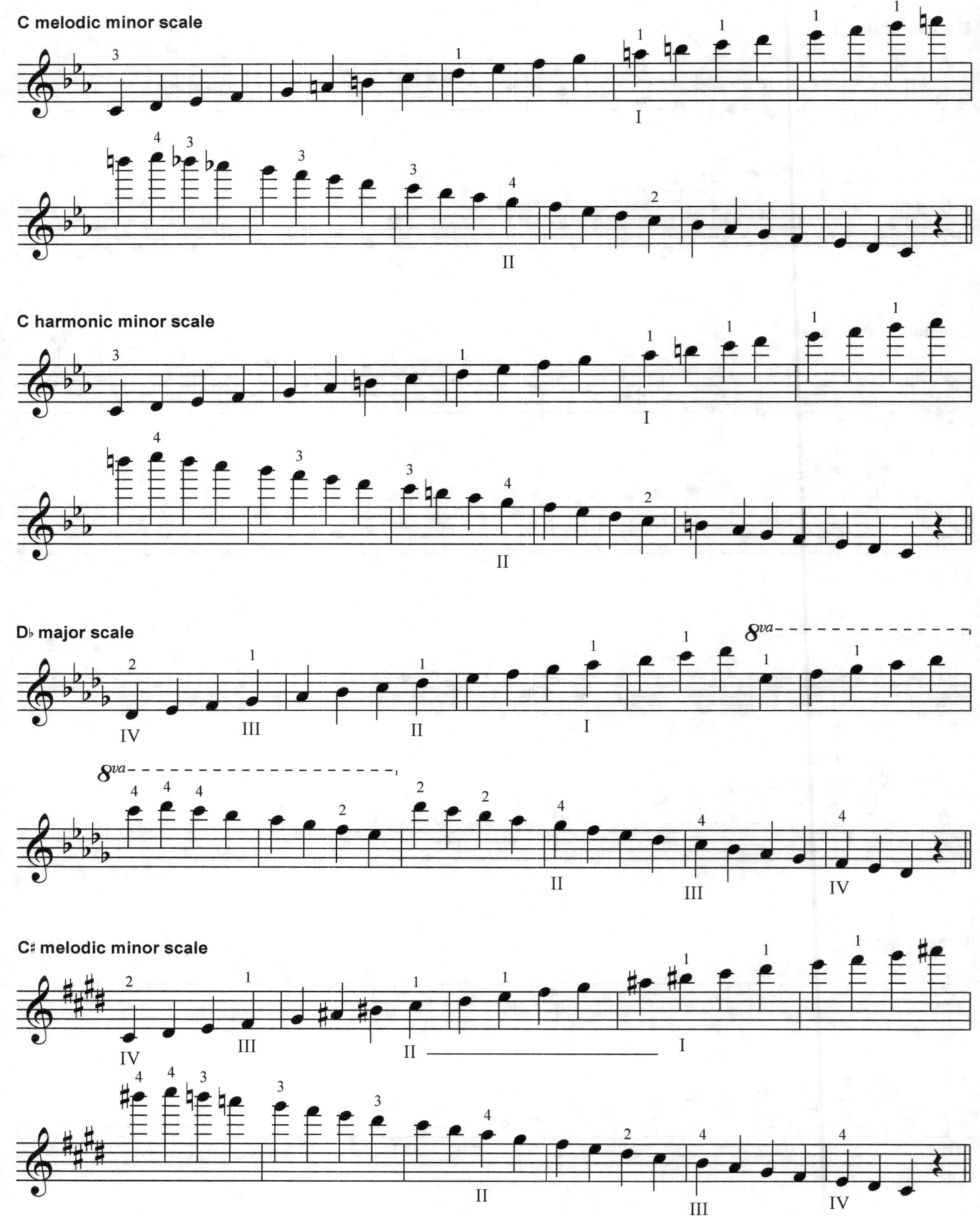

Three-Octave Scales for the Violin, Book One — Complete Scales, Main Fingering 135

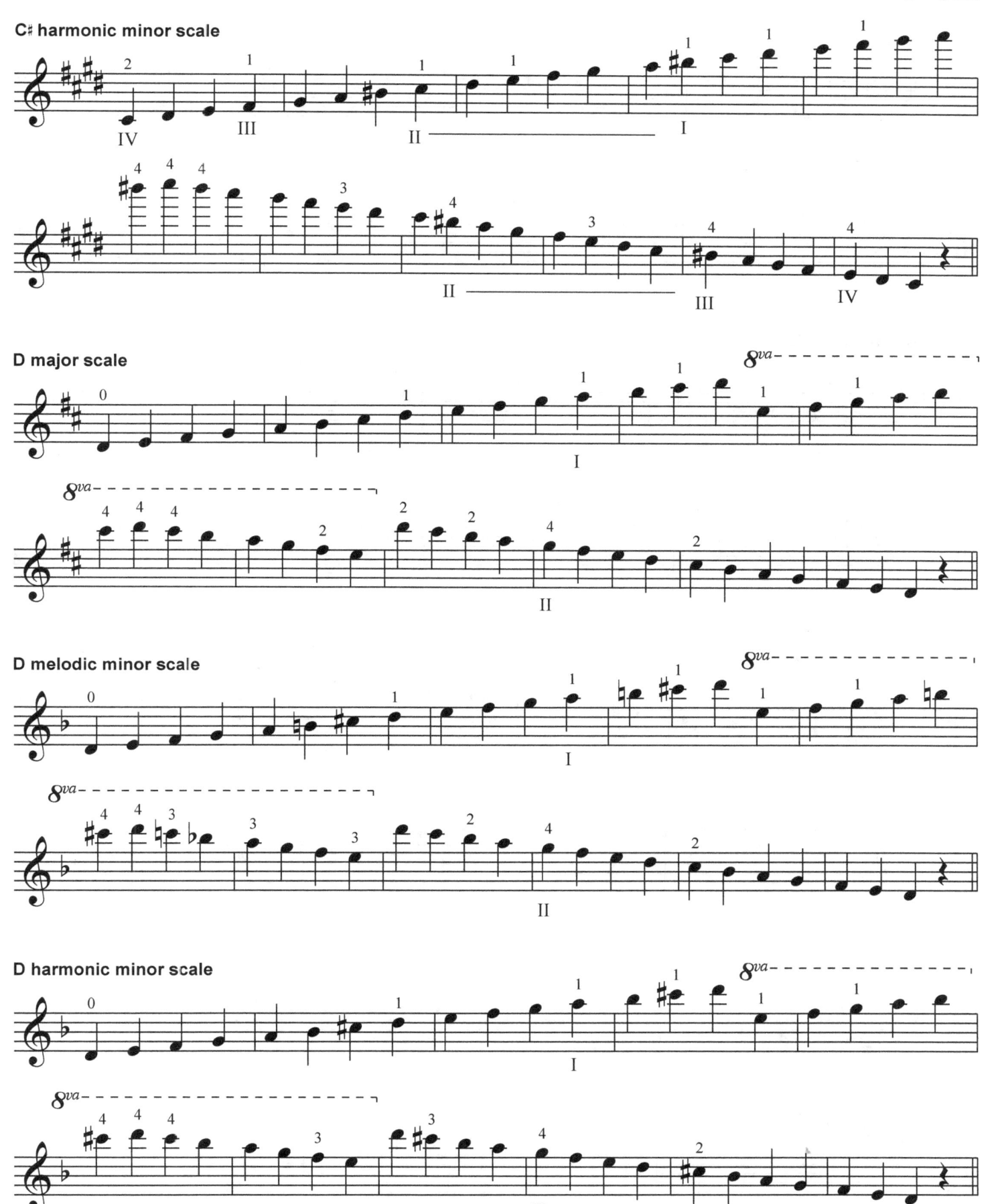

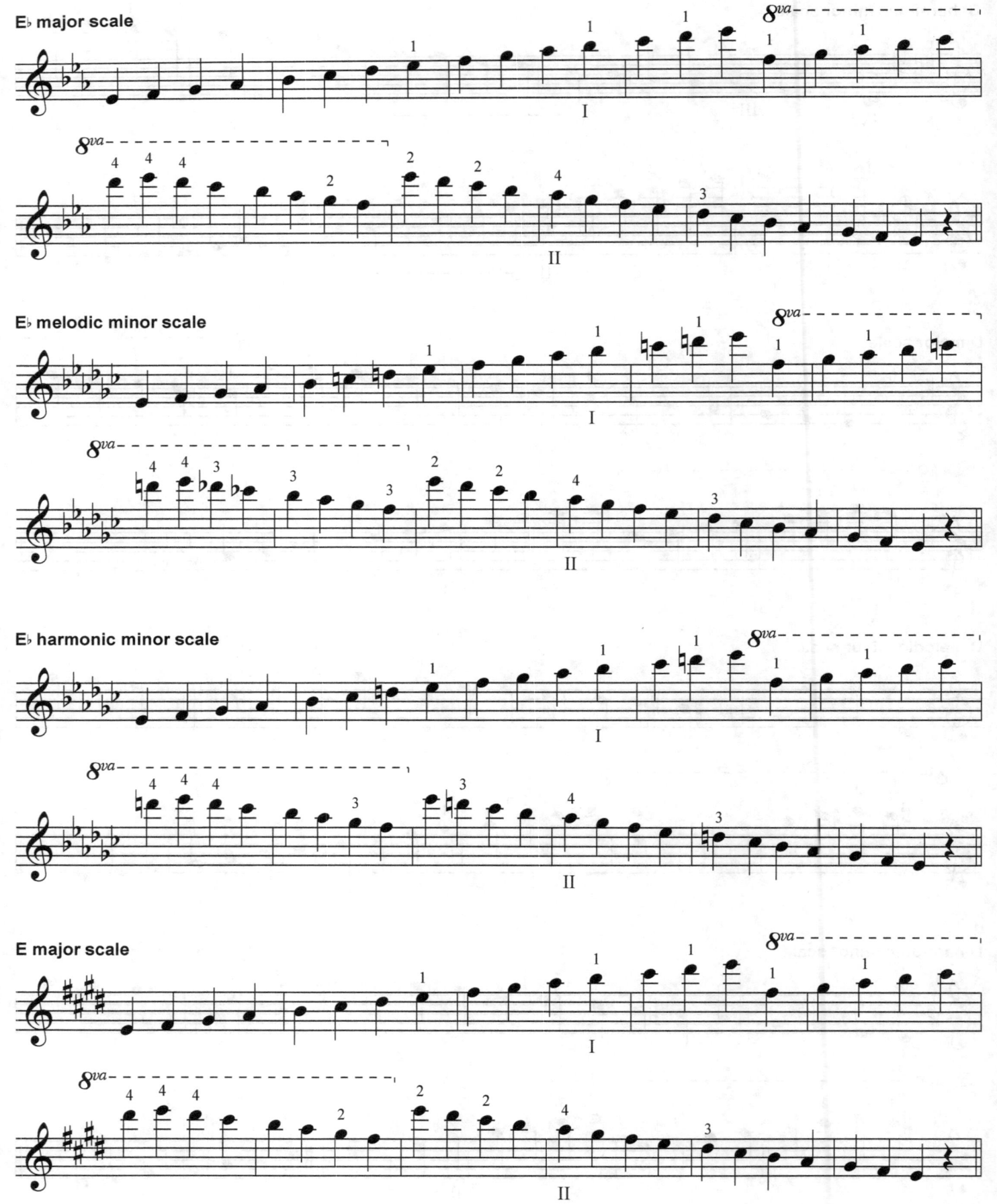

Three-Octave Scales for the Violin, Book One Complete Scales, Main Fingering 137

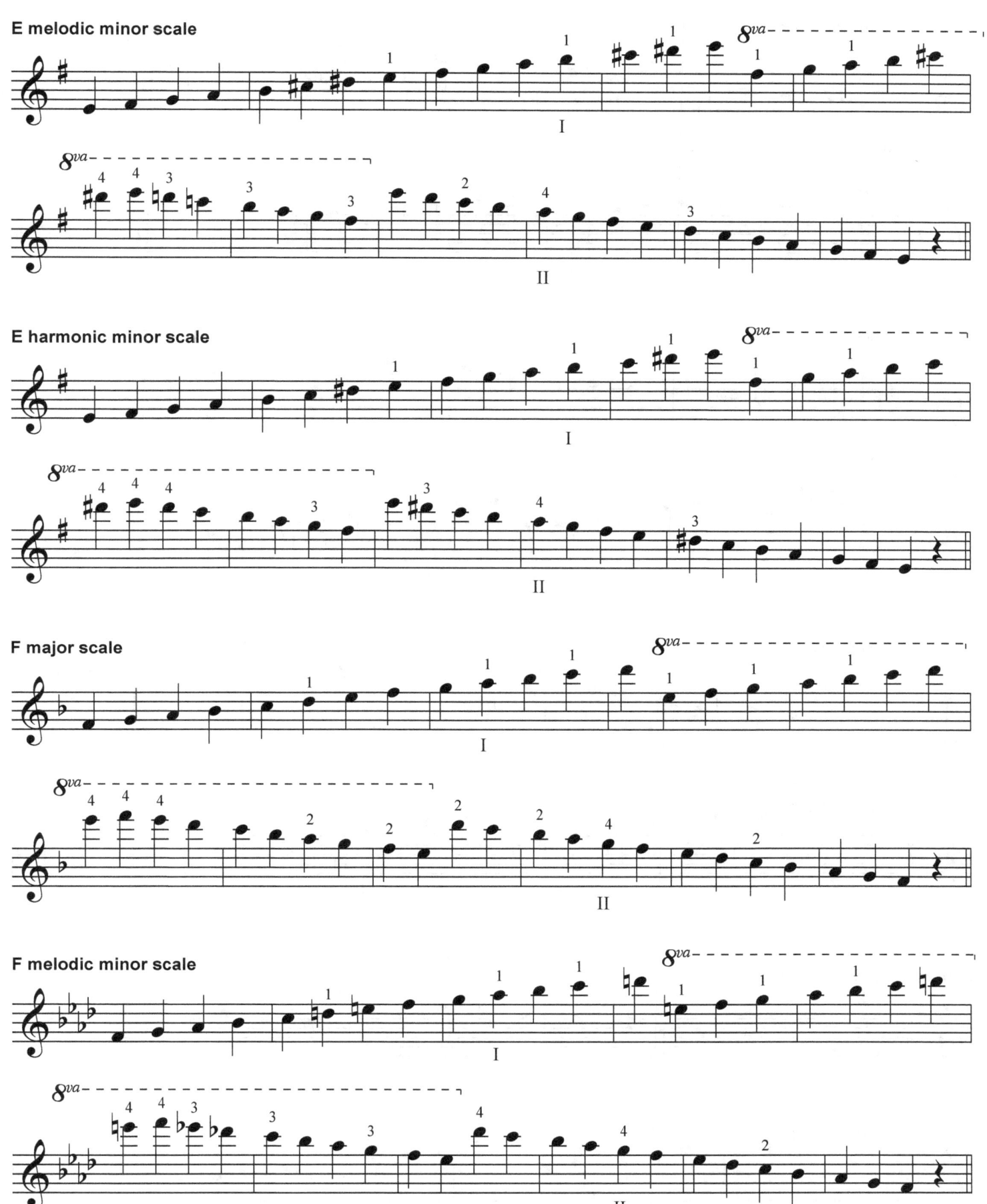

©2019 C. Harvey Publications All Rights Reserved.

Three-Octave Scales for the Violin, Book One

Part Fourteen: Complete Scales, Alternate Fingering

G major scale

G melodic minor scale

G harmonic minor scale

A♭ major scale

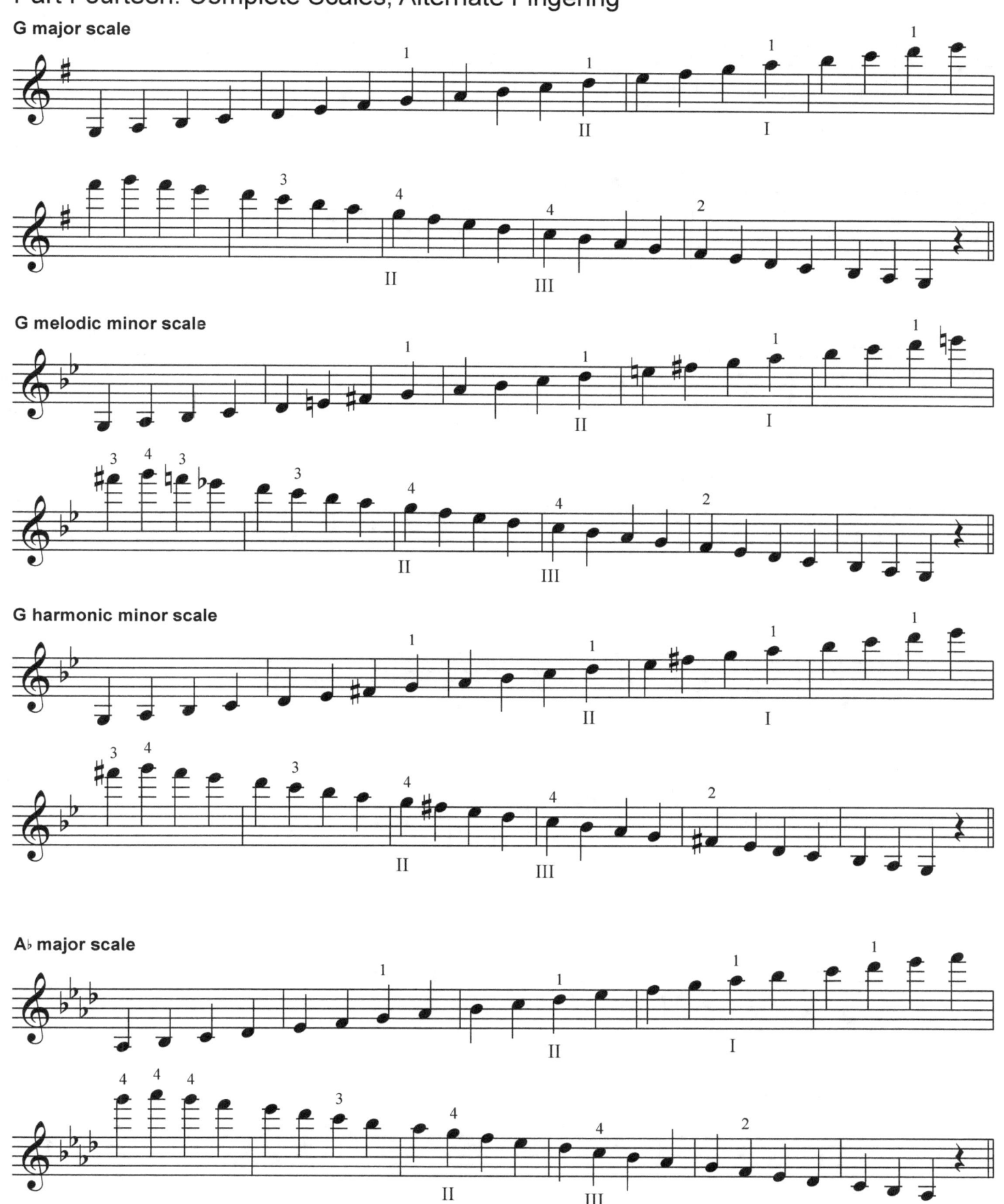

©2019 C. Harvey Publications All Rights Reserved.

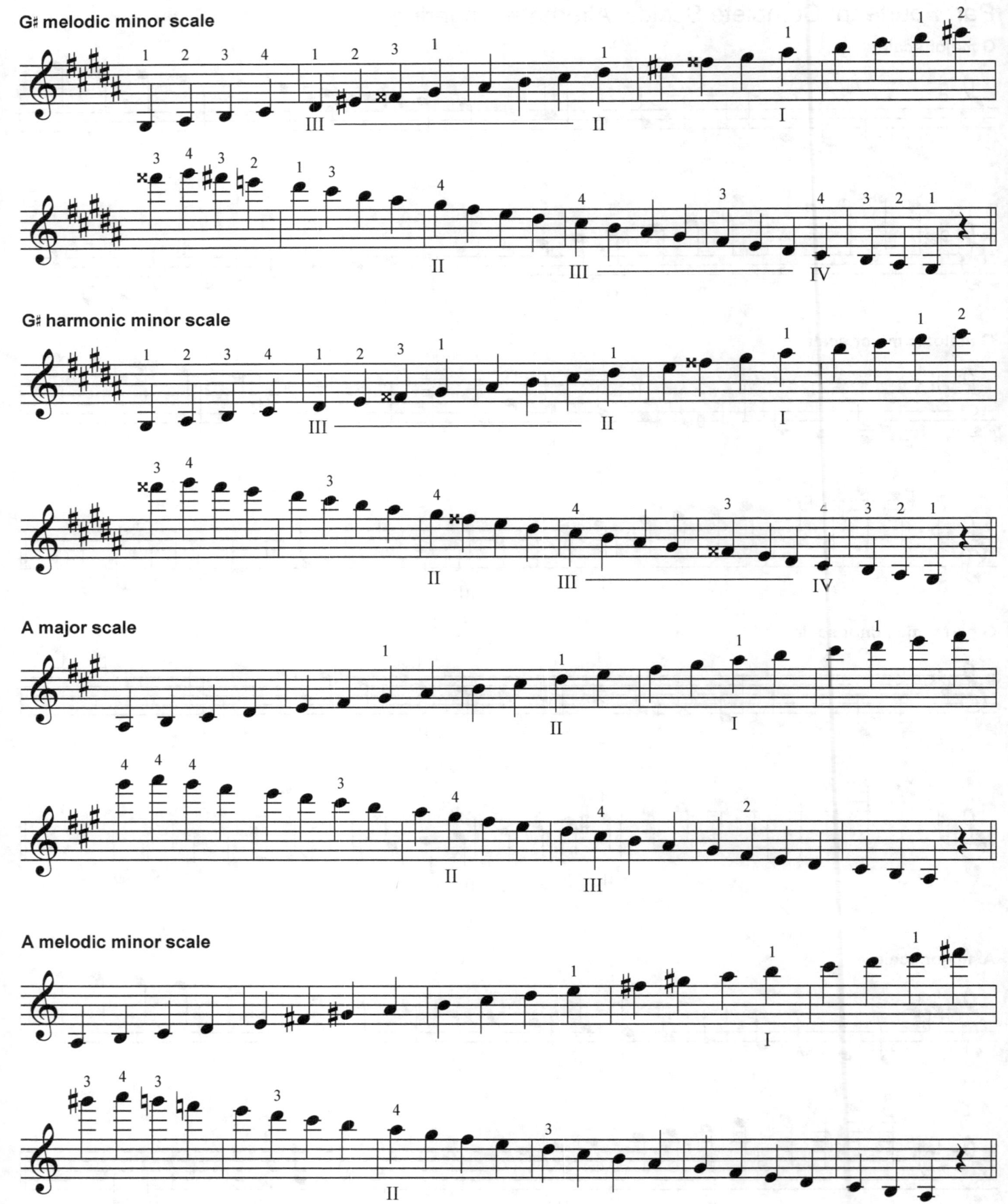

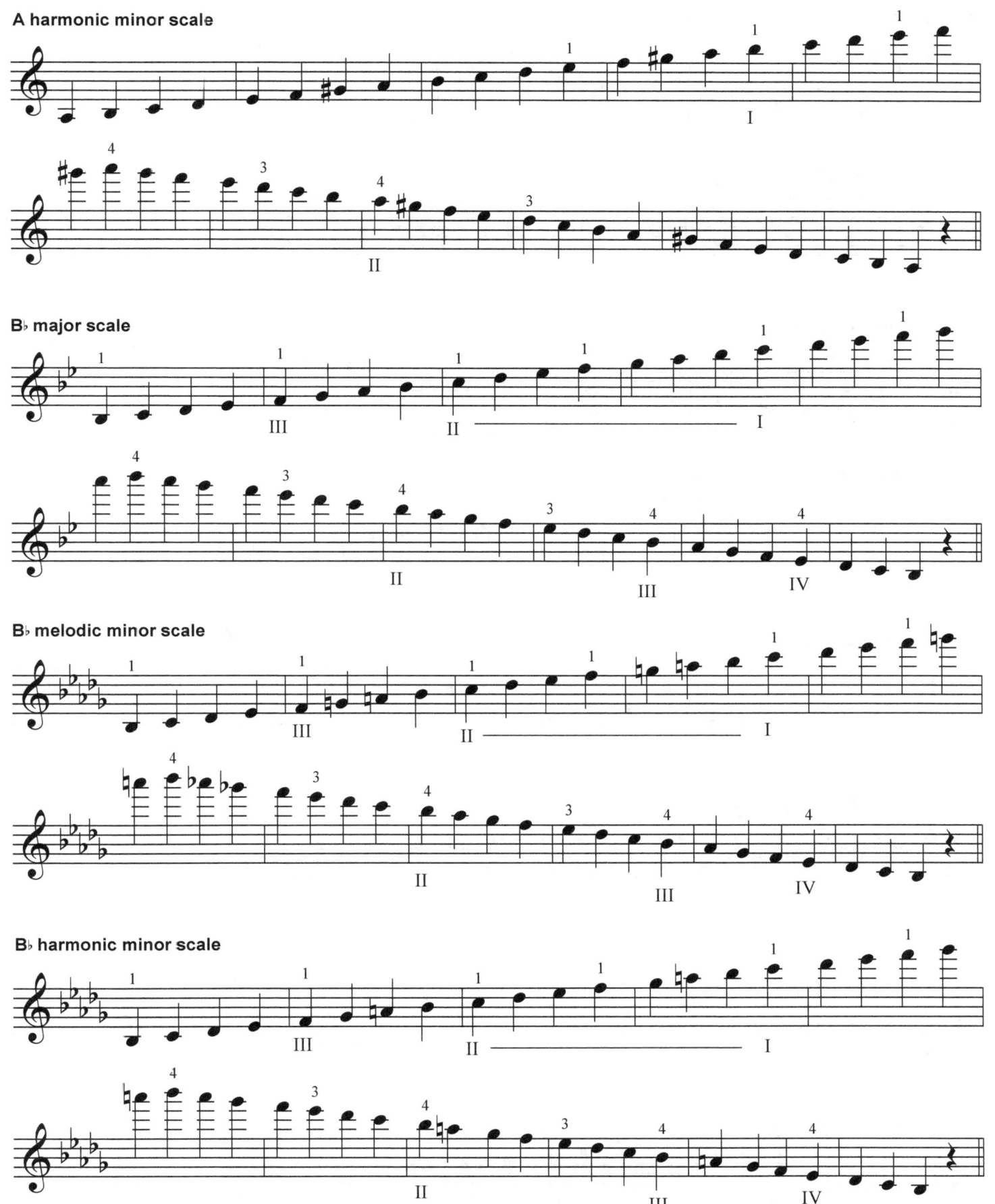

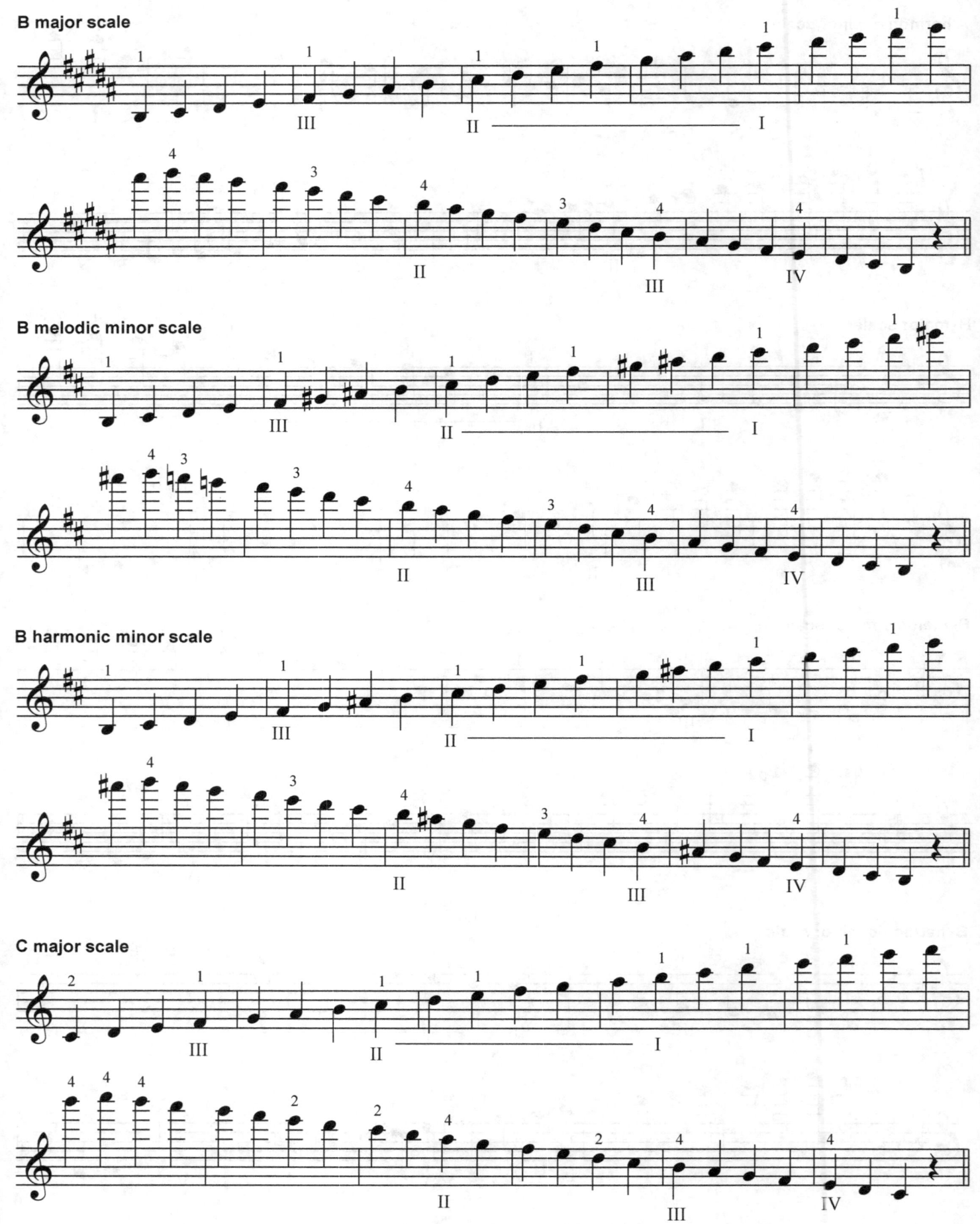

Three-Octave Scales for the Violin, Book One Complete Scales, Alternate Fingering   143

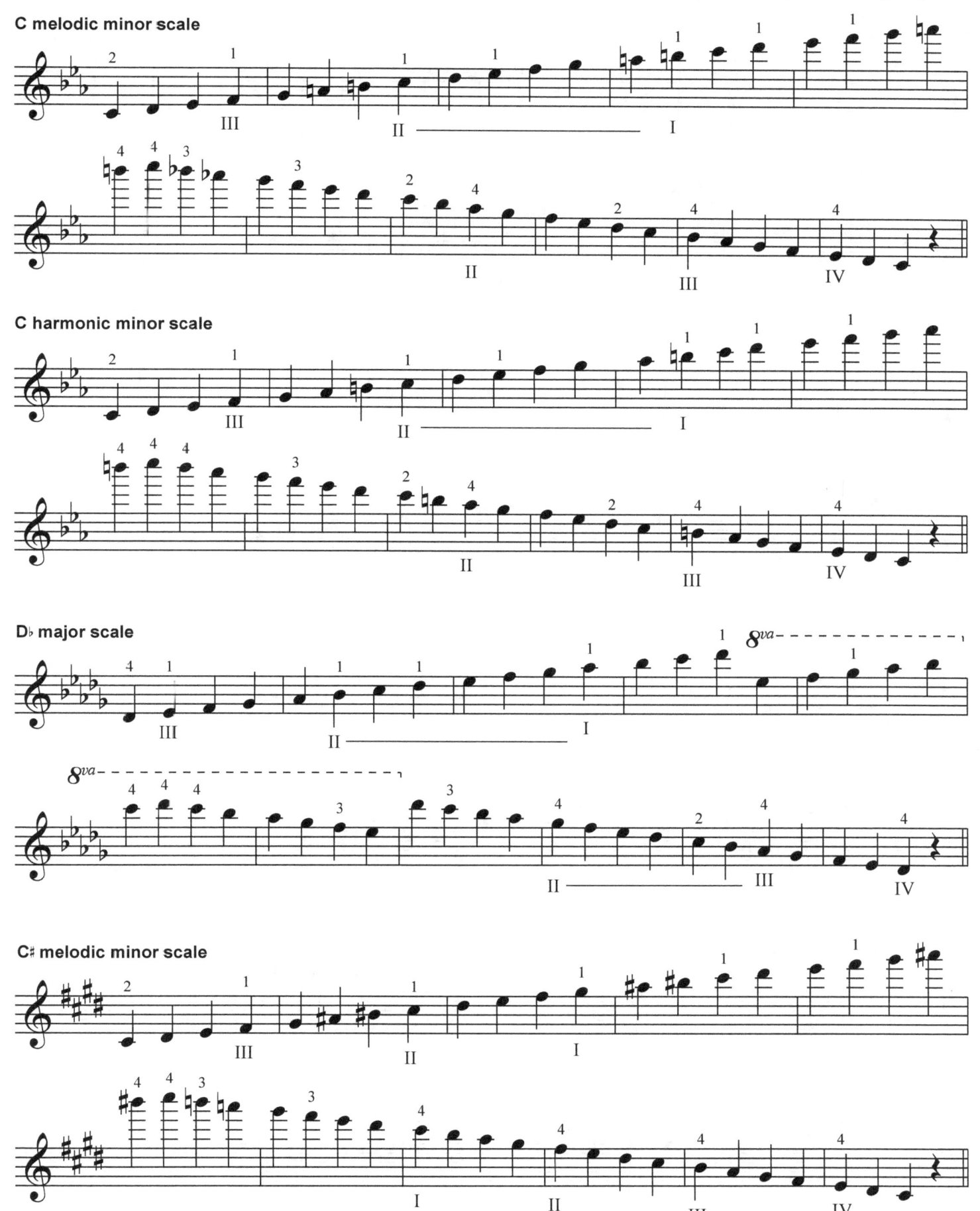

©2019 C. Harvey Publications All Rights Reserved.

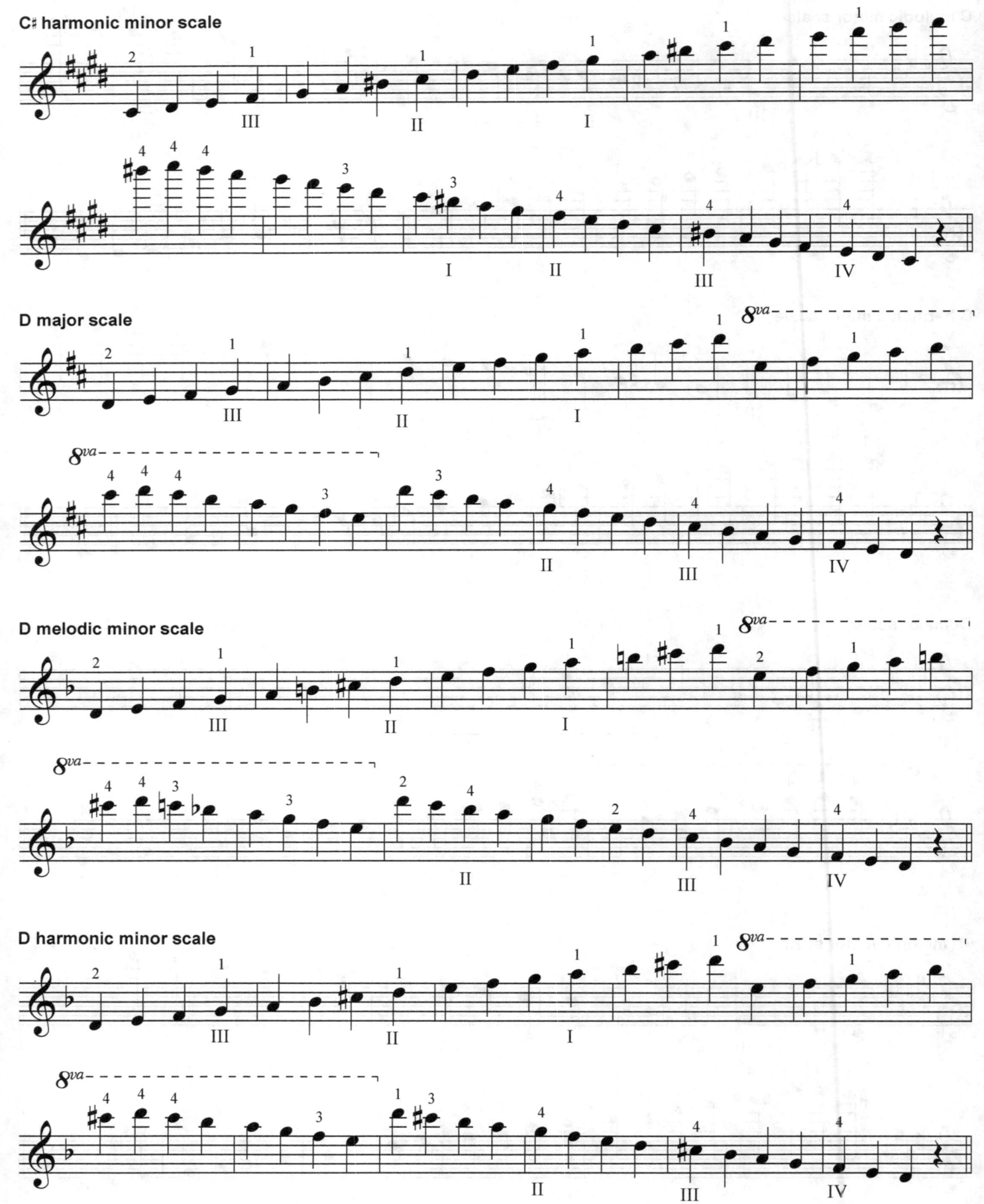

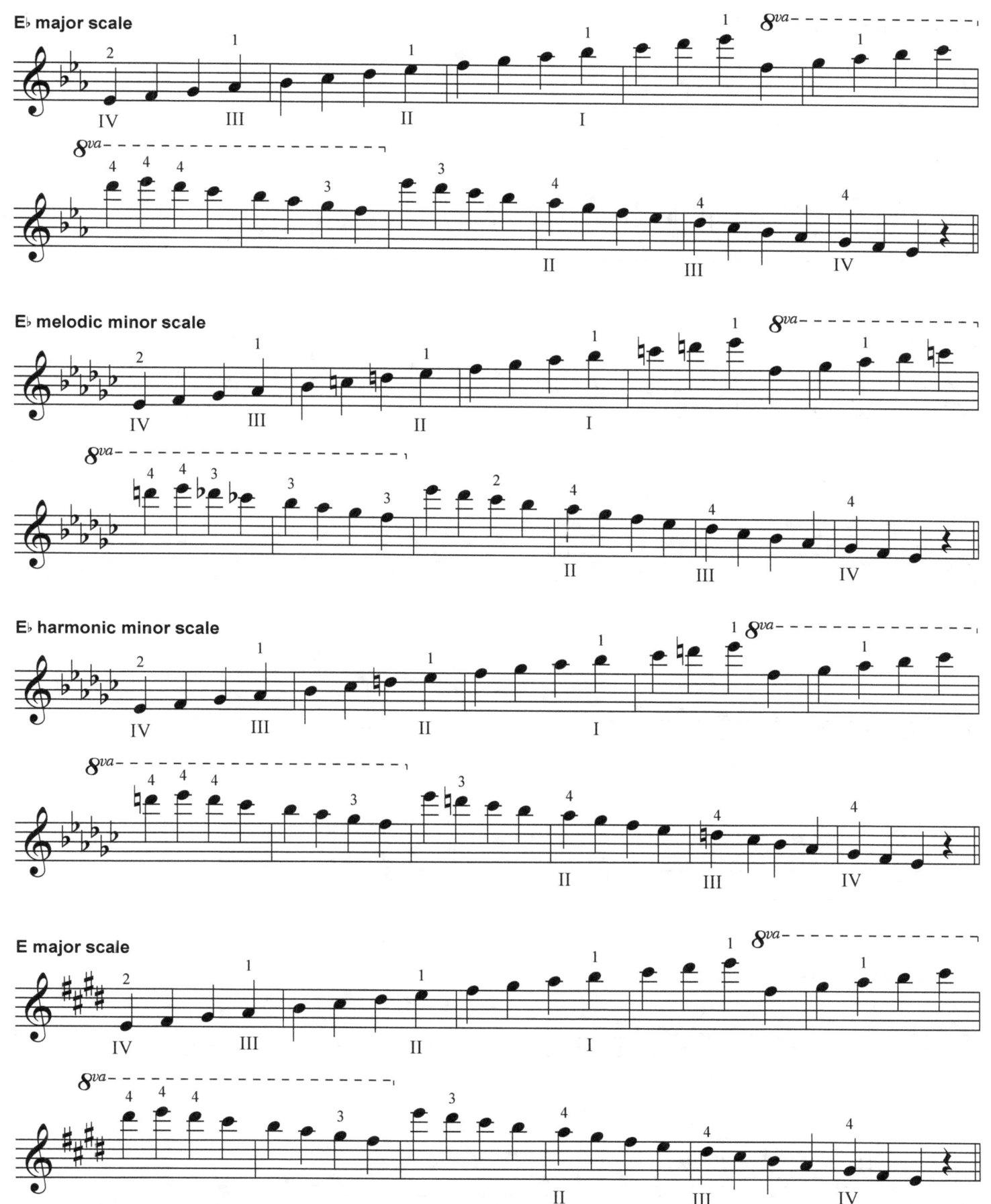

146 Complete Scales, Alternate Fingering Three-Octave Scales for the Violin, Book One

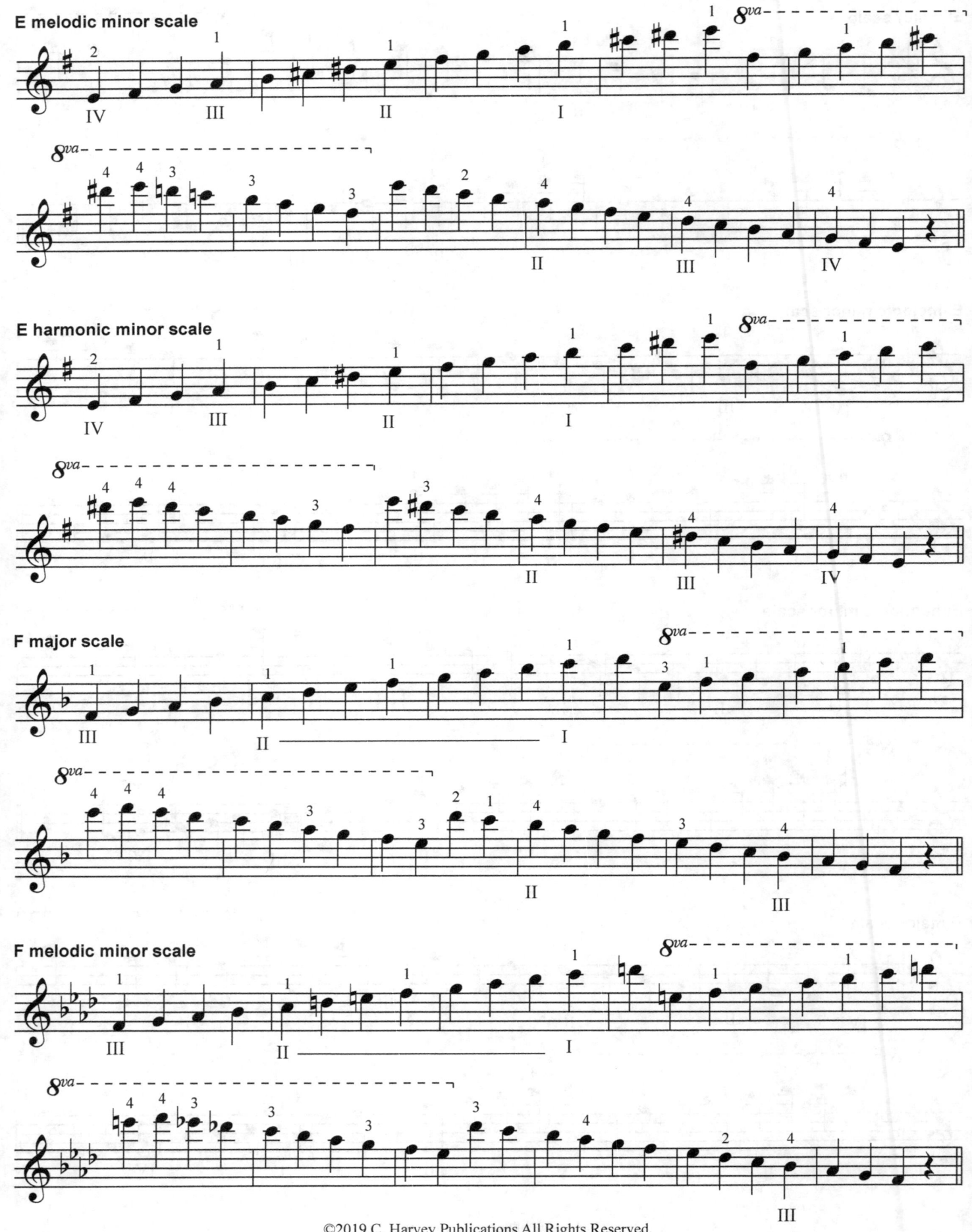

Three-Octave Scales for the Violin, Book One   Complete Scales, Alternate Fingering 147

©2019 C. Harvey Publications All Rights Reserved.

available from **www.charveypublications.com**: CHP178

Scale Studies (One String) for the Violin
Part One: One-Octave Scales
F major

by Cassia Harvey
edited by Myanna Harvey

© 2007 C. Harvey Publications All Rights Reserved.